www.braunconsult.com/careers

**Braun Consulting is a**

**business strategy and**

**technology consulting firm.**

We embrace an

environment that rewards

our employees' unique

perspectives and diverse

backgrounds. We support

collaboration, open

communication, and

feedback. We encourage

creativity and intellectual

curiosity to create innovative

solutions for our clients.

Begin your career with us.

We partner with clients to help

them achieve dramatic

**performance improvement** through

enhanced **customer insight.**

 BraunConsulting

# VAULT CASE INTERVIEW PRACTICE GUIDE

the insider career network™

# VAULT CASE INTERVIEW PRACTICE GUIDE

**RAJIT MALHOTRA, JIM SLEPICKA, SRIKANT BALAN, DEBORAH LIU AND THE STAFF OF VAULT**

# ACKNOWLEDGEMENTS

Vault would like to acknowledge the assistance and support of Matt Doull, Ahmad Al-Khaled, Lee Black, Eric Ober, Hollinger Ventures, Tekbanc, New York City Investment Fund, American Lawyer Media, Globix, Hoover's, Glenn Fischer, Mark Fernandez, Ravi Mhatre, Carter Weiss, Ken Cron, Ed Somekh, Isidore Mayrock, Zahi Khouri, Sana Sabbagh and other Vault investors. Many thanks to our loving families and friends.

Many thanks to Marcy Lerner, Rob Schipano, Val Hadjiyski, Ed Shen, Eric Chung, and Deborah Liu.

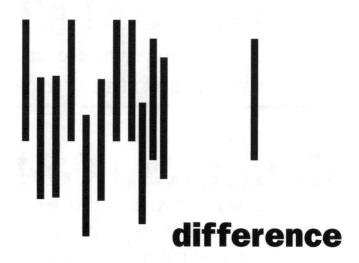

## APPENDIX                                                    125

# INTRODUCTION

# Introduction

If the words "case interview" terrify you, you're in good company. Very few consultants are born as case-crackers: most of the 150,000 or so management consultants sprinkled at this moment across back offices and airport terminals worldwide have faced down the case interview.

The fact is, cases are the primary fortifications around coveted $60,000 undergraduate consulting jobs and plum $110,000 MBA consulting offers for good reason – they work well to predict a candidate's ability to handle the complex and multi-faceted challenges that consultants face every day on the job.

Simply put, the case interview format has evolved to test which element will crack first – you, or the case.

## A special note

If you've bought this book, you're probably already familiar with the *Vault Guide to the Case Interview*. While this guide reviews the essentials of the case and some case frameworks, its primary purpose is to provide additional cases for you to work through. For more in-depth treatment of frameworks and more cases, you should refer to the *Vault Guide to the Case Interview*.

## What is a case?

A case interview is best understood as an interactive, role-playing process. The interviewer pretends to be the client, and you pretend to be a consultant for the firm, exhibiting all the skills, behaviors and competencies that you think consultants at that particular firm should exhibit.

In the most typical format, the interviewer spends under a minute posing a business problem. Few specific details are usually given in this opening – the interviewer then asks a variation on "What would you recommend the client do?" You must then ask logical questions and "move through the problem" to a point where a detailed recommendation can be made.

Interviewers seldom have a specific answer they are searching for – rather, they are keenly interested in assessing your thought process, your industry knowledge, and the delivery style that you employ. Interviewer expectations regarding industry expertise level vary considerably (MBAs and experienced professionals are expected to know more than undergraduates.) However, poise and logical thinking are universally valued in consulting at all levels.

Occasionally, interviewers will create a case on the spot, tailored to the candidate's background. (They'll probably do this by looking at your resume.) In this situation, the interviewer often has similar project experience and is most likely looking to judge the candidate's business acumen to assess the depth of thinking on a given business problem.

## Why the case?

Simply put, the case interview is a unique and challenging interview format because the role of a consultant is a distinctly rigorous profession.

Consultants are not paid to work in a bubble – consultants typically spend over 90 percent of their billable hours interacting directly with clients or working on-site at the client organization. This reality places a premium on "presenting well" to the client while grinding through thorny business problems worthy of billing time at several hundred dollars per hour.

"Presenting well" to clients can best be described as a series of seemingly contradictory skills. In the words of one expert, a consultant must "be cool under pressure, be influential without being condescending, have the ability to understand granular aspects of a problem while simultaneously aggregating them into the big picture, and have the ability to self-police a balance between personal and professional lifestyle." This tall order is to be filled in an extremely turbulent work environment with "nonstop engagement team changes, hostile client environments, countless political influences and near-perpetual travel."

Perhaps most difficult to bear in the long term, consultants must derive enough personal satisfaction from their working lives to put up with a lack of psychological and practical support, including normal workplace standards such as a permanent working space, the ability to return home each night, easy access to administrative services and the camaraderie that develops among co-workers assigned to the same business unit. In the face of all this, consultants must remain cheerful, alert and helpful. And these same qualities must be conveyed in the case interview. Let's get to it!

# Do you have an interview coming up with a consulting firm?

# Unsure how to handle a case interview?

## Vault Live Case Interview Prep

Vault's consulting experts bring you a new service to help you prepare for interviews with consulting firms. We'll help you prepare for that all-important case interview with a 30-minute mock interview and a 30-minute question and answer session with our consulting expert over the telephone.

A Vault consulting expert will put you through a real case used by the major consulting firms. You will be given the case at your appointment and will be asked to explain it, dissect it, and give a rationale for your responses.

### The prep session will cover:

- Case strategies for attacking different case types
- Case frameworks, including Value Chain Analysis and Value Drivers Frameworks
- Market sizing cases
- A representative business strategy case (for example, a market-entry case)
- And more!

## For more information go to http://consulting.vault.com

# CASE INTERVIEW BASICS: CASE TYPES AND SKILLS

# Case Types

The case interview format is highly versatile and freely adapted by seasoned consultants. Nonetheless, most case interviews fall into one of three categories: business cases, guesstimates and brainteasers. For the most part, this guide will cover the first, business cases (otherwise simply known as cases.)

## Business cases

The business case is the classic and most common format for case interviews. A business scenario is presented and you are asked to perform an analysis and make recommendations. The vast majority of business cases are executed through an interactive, verbal exchange. In some cases the interviewee will receive a sheet of paper with several columns of financial data (see note on "Basic Interpretation of Financial Statements," below), or a set of several PowerPoint slides. (Undergraduates: in case you've never worked with PowerPoint before, you might want to familiarize yourself with the program before your interview.) Most often, however, a blank notepad is the only lifeline you will have to work with. You should bring this notepad with you. It's also smart to bring a calculator – you may not be allowed to use it, but if you are, you will be happy you brought it.

## Guesstimates

"Back-of-the-envelope" calculations are an essential element of most business cases. (If you hadn't guessed, this term refers to off-the-cuff calculations.) If you have made good progress in framing key aspects of a business scenario and are proceeding towards a recommendation, the interviewer may suddenly interject with some "new data" from the client and request that you determine the implications for your analysis.

For undergraduate hires and graduate-level candidates whose quantitative skills are perceived to be weak, a guesstimate may be converted into a "stand-alone" case interview. In the classic example, the interviewee is asked to estimate the number of pingpong balls that would fit inside a 747 airplane.

As with more general business cases, there is almost never an exact answer, but there are plenty of wrong answers. What makes a good answer? Interviewers will note whether you've come close, and most importantly, will note whether you've used a logical process and have clearly stated your assumptions along the way. The trick is to strike a good balance between estimates that are reasonably accurate while using numbers that are convenient to handle in your head or on paper. (Even if you come to a close-to-correct answer while silently doing calculations in your head, your interviewer may just think you've guessed correctly, so make sure to elucidate your logic as you solve the guesstimate.)

**In the case of the pingpong balls in the 747 example, a process both logical and convenient would be as follows:**

1. Establish a reasonable estimate for the size of a pingpong ball (1.5 inches in diameter).

2. Establish a convenient estimate for the number of pingpong balls in a "standard unit" of space. (For example, let's say you can fit eight pingpong balls in one foot. Determine the volume of pingpong balls in a cubic foot – eight cubed – and you get 512.).

3. Move on to estimating the cubic feet of volume inside a 747 plane. Here you could get more creative, using one of several options. You could focus on the inside of the plane, taking an estimated number of cabin passengers in each section and multiplying by the amount of seat and overhead luggage space for coach, business-class and first-class customers. Or you could work with the outside dimensions of the plane, visualizing the cabin of the plane as a cylinder and applying the formula for calculating volume.

4. Divide the volume of the 747 by the number of cubic feet, and multiply by 512 to get the number of pingpong balls.

5. You're not done yet! To demonstrate your thoroughness, go back to step 3 and use one of the alternative estimating methods to cross-check your answer. Having the presence of mind to be both creative and thorough is something that interviewers will carefully watch for.

## Brainteasers

A less common form of case interviews, brainteasers are akin to riddles or logic puzzles and are often timed to gauge the candidate's ability to combine creative thinking with poise. Brainteasers are more common on the undergrad-recruiting scene and are rarer in business school interviews.

Brainteasers typically come in two forms. The "creative" kind is shorter and is done without calculations. The "less-fun" kind (for most consultants at least) resembles a math problem and requires more time and calculations. As you might expect, math brainteasers are often used for positions where mathematical aptitude is crucial.

**The classic example of a "creative" brainteaser is:**
"Give me three reasons why manhole covers are round."

*Here are some sample answers to this question, though there are many others.*

• It's easier to dig round shafts into the ground than square shafts.

• One person can transport a round cover (by rolling) but two must carry a square cover.

• A round cover can't fall through the hole. It's safer.

**An example of a mathematical brainteaser is:**
"The area and volume of a certain sphere are both four-digit integers times pi. What is the radius of the sphere?"

*Here's how you figure it out.*

Area $= 4 \pi r^2$, and given that $4 r^2$ is a 4-digit integer.

Volume $= 4/3 \pi r^3$ and $4/3 r^3$ is also a 4-digit integer.

Observe that since $4 r^2$ is an integer, $4/3 r^3 = (4 r^2)*(r/3)$ is also an integer, whereby it follows that r is a multiple of 3, to ensure that $(r/3)$ is an integer.

Substitute $r = 3, 6, 9, 12, 15, 18$, and Bingo! R = 18 is the only value that satisfies the two conditions.

**For both types of problem, several general guidelines apply:**

1. If your thoughts freeze at the start of the problem, do not stumble. Pause. Ask for a moment to collect your thoughts. Scribble on your note pad, if that helps you. Only then should you outline your thought process for the interviewer. Even if you can't get anywhere near a solution, you can salvage a "pass" from the interviewer if you stay cool and demonstrate an ability to break apart the problem.

2. If you get lost midway toward a solution, go back through your process and attempt to rework your way through your stages of analysis. This will help you get your bearings.

3. While the format of brainteasers is often lighthearted, take care to demonstrate a professional and analytical approach. Interviewers are looking for calm, deliberate thinking, not goofiness and guesswork.

# Analyzing Financial Statements

Full-fledged financial statement analysis is a subject requiring extensive experience and training, but every case interviewee should be equipped with a working knowledge of the four snapshots of a firm's financial position: the Income Statement, the Balance Sheet, the Statement of Retained Earnings, and the Statement of Cash Flows (names of financial statements are capitalized).

## Interpretation for management

Case interviews will never require you to perform hands-on accounting analysis. You will, however, be expected to quickly glance at accounting statements and develop a "back of the envelope" interpretation of the data for your interviewer.

The key to success in this endeavor is twofold. First, you must possess the fluency in accounting statements (and learning accounting really is similar to learning a language) to quickly spot areas of concern. Second, you should be able to quickly link the financial data back to a case analysis framework that answers the original question presented to you by the interviewer.

To facilitate your ability to quickly interpret the financial statements outlined above, it's very helpful to work from a framework of key questions. Following is a basic outline of key points to consider when translating raw accounting information from financial statements to your case interviewer.

# Basic Overview of Financial Statements

Even if you're not an MBA, many consulting firms — especially those with strong financial consulting bents — will expect you to have some comprehension of basic financial statements. If you haven't studied accounting, don't panic – these statements are relatively easy to understand.

There are four basic financial statements that provide the information needed to evaluate a company. They include:

- The Balance Sheet
- The Income Statement
- The Statements of Retained Earnings
- The Statements of Cash Flows

In addition, a company's annual report is almost always accompanied by notes to the financial statements. These notes provide additional information about the numbers provided in the four basic financial statements.

The next four sections provide a general overview of the four basic financial statements.

## The Balance Sheet

The Balance Sheet presents the financial position of a company at a given point in time. It is comprised of three parts: Assets, Liabilities and Equity. (Like the statements themselves, the accounts in financial statements are capitalized.) Assets are the economic resources of a company. They are the resources that the company uses to operate its business and include Cash, Inventory and Equipment. A company normally obtains the resources it uses to operate its business by incurring debt, obtaining new investors, or through operating earnings. The Liabilities section of the Balance Sheet presents the debts of the company. Liabilities are the claims that creditors have on the company's resources. The Equity section of the Balance Sheet presents the net worth of a company, which equals the assets that the company owns less the debts they owe to creditors. Equity can also be defined as the claims that investors have on the company's resources.

This example uses the basic format of a Balance Sheet:

### Media Entertainment, Inc
Balance Sheet
December 31, 2003

| Assets | | Liabilities | |
|---|---|---|---|
| Cash | 203,000 | Accounts Payable | 7,000 |
| Accounts Receivable | 26,000 | | |
| Building | 19,000 | **Equity** | |
| | | Common Stock | 10,000 |
| | | Retained Earnings | 231,000 |
| | | | |
| **Total Assets** | 248,000 | **Total Liabilities & Equity** | 248,000 |

Because a company can obtain resources from both investors and creditors, one must be able to distinguish between the two and understand why one type is classified as a Liability and the other type is classified as Equity. Companies incur debt to obtain the economic resources necessary to operate their businesses and promise to pay the debt back over a specified period of time. This promise to pay is fixed and is not based upon the operating performance of the company. Companies also seek new investors to obtain economic resources. However, they don't promise to pay investors back a specified amount over a specified period of time. Instead, companies promise investors a return on their investment that is often contingent upon a certain level of operating performance. Since an equity holder's investment is not guaranteed, it is more risky in nature than a loan made by a creditor. But if a company performs well, the return to investors is often higher. The "promise-to-pay" element makes loans made by creditors a Liability and, as an accountant would say, more "senior" than equity holdings.

To summarize, the Balance Sheet represents the economic resources of a business, including the claims that creditors and equity holders have on those resources. Debts owed to creditors are more senior than the investments of equity holders and are classified as Liabilities, while equity investments are accounted for in the Equity section of the Balance Sheet.

## The Income Statement

We have discussed two of the three ways in which a company normally obtains the economic resources necessary to operate its business: incurring debt and seeking new investors. A third way in which a company can obtain resources is through its own operations. The Income Statement presents the results of operations of a business over a specified period of time (e.g., one year, one quarter, one month) and is comprised of Revenues, Expenses and Net Income.

**Revenue:** Revenue is a source of income that normally arises from the sale of goods or services and is recorded when it is earned. For example, when a retailer of roller blades makes a sale, the sale would be considered revenue. However, revenue may also come from other sources. For example, selling a business segment or a piece of capital equipment generates a type of revenue for a company. This type of income would be considered a gain on sale. Gains are sources of income from peripheral or incidental transactions (all economic events that are not usual and frequent).

**Expenses:** Expenses are the costs incurred by a business over a specified period of time to generate the revenues earned during that same period of time. For example, in order for a manufacturing company to sell a product, it must buy the materials it needs to make the product. In addition, that same company must pay people to both make and sell the product. The company must also pay salaries to the individuals who operate the business. These are all types of expenses that a company can incur during the normal operations of the business. When a company incurs an expense outside of its normal operations, it is considered a "loss." Losses are expenses incurred as a result of one-time or incidental transactions. The destruction of office equipment in a fire, for example, would be a loss.

Incurring expenses and acquiring assets both involve the use of economic resources (i.e., cash or debt). So, when is a purchase considered an asset, and when is it considered an expense?

**Assets vs. expenses:** A purchase is considered an asset if it provides future economic benefit to the company, while expenses only relate to the current period. For example, monthly salaries paid to employees for services that they already provided during the month would be considered expenses. On the other hand, the purchase of a piece of manufacturing equipment would be classified as an asset, as it will probably be used to manufacture a product for more than one accounting period.

**Net Income:** The revenue a company earns, less its expenses during a specified period of time, equals its net income. A positive net income number indicates a profit, while a negative net income number indicates that a company suffered a loss (called a "net loss").

Here is an example of an Income Statement:

## Media Entertainment, Inc
Income Statement
(For the year ended December 31, 2003)

| Revenues | | |
|---|---|---|
| Services Billed | | 100,000 |
| | | |
| Expenses | | |
| Salaries and Wages | (33,000) | |
| Rent Expense | (17,000) | |
| Utilities Expense | (7,000) | (57,000) |
| Net Income | | 43,000 |

To summarize, the Income Statement measures the success of a company's operations; it provides investors and creditors with information to determine the profitability and creditworthiness of the enterprise. A company has earned net income when its total revenues exceed its total expenses. A company has a net loss when total expenses exceed total revenues.

## The Statement of Retained Earnings

The Statement of Retained Earnings is a reconciliation of the Retained Earnings account from the beginning to the end of the year. When a company announces income or declares dividends, this information is reflected in the Statement of Retained Earnings. Net income increases the Retained Earnings account. Net losses and dividend payments decrease Retained Earnings.

Here is an example of a basic Statement of Retained Earnings:

### Media Entertainment, Inc
Statement of Retained Earnings
(For the year ended December 31, 2003)

| | |
|---|---|
| **Retained Earnings, January 1, 2003** | $200,000 |
| **Plus:** Net income for the year | 43,000 |
| | 243,000 |
| | |
| **Less:** Dividends declared | (12,000) |
| | |
| **Retained Earnings, December 31, 2003** | $ 231,000 |

As you can probably tell by looking at this example, the Statement of Retained Earnings doesn't provide any new information not already reflected in other financial statements. But it does provide additional information about what management is doing with the company's earnings. Management may be "plowing back" the company's net income into the business by retaining part or all of its earnings, distributing its current income to shareholders, or distributing current and accumulated income to shareholders. (Investors can use this information to align their investment strategy with the strategy of a company's management. An investor interested in growth and returns on capital may be more inclined to invest in a company that "plows back" its resources into the company for the purpose of generating additional resources. Conversely, an investor interested in receiving current income is more inclined to invest in a company that pays quarterly dividend distributions to shareholders.)

## The Statement of Cash Flows

Remember that the Income Statement provides information about the economic resources involved in the operation of a company. However, the Income Statement does not provide information about the actual source and use of cash generated during its operations. That's because obtaining and using economic resources doesn't always involve cash. For example, let's say you went shopping and bought a new mountain bike on your credit card in July, but didn't pay the bill until August. Although the store did not receive cash in July, the sale would still be considered July revenue. The Statement of Cash Flows presents a detailed summary of all of the cash inflows and outflows during the period and is divided into three sections based on three types of activity:

- **Cash flows from operating activities:** includes the cash effects of transactions involved in calculating net income

- **Cash flows from investing activities:** involves items classified as assets in the Balance Sheet and includes the purchase and sale of equipment and investments

- **Cash flows from financing activities:** involves items classified as liabilities and equity in the Balance Sheet; it includes the payment of dividends as well as issuing payment of debt or equity

Here is an example that shows the basic format of the Statement of Cash Flows:

## Media Entertainment, Inc
### Statement of Cash Flows
### For the year ended December 31, 2003

| | | |
|---|---:|---:|
| **Cash flows provided from operating activities** | | |
| Net Income | 33,000 | |
| Depreciation Expense | 10,000 | |
| Increase in Accounts Receivable | (26,000) | |
| Increase in Accounts Payable | 7,000 | (9,000) |
| **Net cash provided by operating activities** | 24,000 | |
| **Cash flows provided from investing activities** | | |
| Purchase of Building | (19,000) | |
| Sale of Long-Term Investment | 35,000 | |
| **Net cash provided by investing activities** | 16,000 | |
| **Cash flows provided from financing activities** | | |
| Payment of Dividends | (12,000) | |
| Issuance of Common Stock | 10,000 | |
| **Net cash provided by financing activities** | (2,000) | |
| **Net increase (decrease) in cash** | 38,000 | |
| **Cash at the beginning of the year** | 165,000 | |
| **Cash at the end of the year** | 203,000 | |

As you can tell by looking at the above example, the Statement of Cash Flows gets its information from all three of the other financial statements:

• Net income from the Income Statement is shown in the section "cash flows from operating activities."

• Dividends from the Statement of Retained Earnings is shown in the section "cash flows from financing activities."

• Investments, Accounts Payable, and other asset and liability accounts from the Balance Sheet are shown in all three sections.

# How Tough Will It Be?

The old maxim "Prepare for the worst, and hope for the best" applies. The level of difficulty of your case is highly unpredictable and subject to random variables such as the background and personality of your interviewer.

The setting and context for cases is the most predictable determinant of format. There are significant differences between undergraduate-level and MBA-level cases. Undergraduates with significant business experience, as well as non-MBA graduate students with significant quantitative experience, may get cases closer to the MBA level.

## Cases for undergraduates

Generally, undergrad candidates will receive more guidance from the interviewer, if they ask for it. Numerical computations for undergrads are normally in the form of guesstimates rather than integrated into the case. If numbers are given to undergrads, they will usually be in a very structured format.

Undergrad cases tend to emphasize qualitative analysis and critical thinking, with a de-emphasis on business acumen, financial statement analysis, etc. Most importantly, one case framework is typically all that's needed to crack an undergrad case.

## Cases for MBAs

Interviewers crank up the pressure on MBAs through several tactics. For one, the format and information flow in MBA cases is usually very open-ended – the interviewee is fully responsible for controlling the course of the case. Financial data given to the candidate is usually on the cryptic side – candidates must typically ask questions to verify where the data comes from, how it is trending, and then move on to interpret the data in a manner consistent with management's objectives.

Interviewers further spice up the open-ended format by introducing a sudden change in the data, e.g., "Let's assume the factory is in China and not in Mexico." MBA candidates are expected to turn on a dime and reassess all the variables and assumptions that led the case discussion to the point where the change was introduced.

Last but not least, the combination of open-ended format and sudden changes mandates that MBA candidates be prepared to apply more than one case framework to a given problem. The most "polished" case-crackers are able to silently shift gears and weave insightful recommendations into a comprehensive-sounding framework of analysis.

# Skills Assessed in the Case Interview

The first step to becoming a top case-cracker is to fully understand the hidden agenda behind the exercise. From the interviewer's perspective, Agenda Item No. 1 is to get behind the two-dimensional snapshot provided by your resume. Even the best-written resume is only capable of getting you in the door. The case interview is the firm's chance to take the product marketed by your resume (you) out for a test drive.

In almost all cases, interviewers will evaluate your performance on two basic dimensions: analytics and client/team Skills. The analytics dimension will probe your facility with numbers, your logic, business judgment and focus. The client and team skills dimension will assess your energy, composure and professionalism under pressure, as well as communication, leadership and teamwork skills.

## Applying a "Balanced Scorecard" approach

Since many cases are delivered as part of large on-campus recruiting visits involving many consultants, most firms employ a standard evaluation form to ensure consistency in evaluating candidates.

In general, your goal is twofold: you should aim to ensure all boxes are checked for each of these key areas, and aim to exceed expectations in several of them.

The following list represents a comprehensive "wish list" of key traits distilled from insiders from a range of leading firms:

# Analytics

Many professionals are accustomed to thinking of analytical skills as either qualitative or quantitative. While this dichotomy holds up well in many fields, case interview evaluation is a unique world with a unique set of rules.

## Quantitative skills

Be prepared to run some numbers for your case interviews – and be prepared to do it at a moment's notice at the whim of your interviewer. No matter what type of consultant position you're interviewing for, be prepared to roll up your sleeves for some numerical computations.

This is one of the most "straightforward" areas you will be evaluated on, but for many it is one of the hardest areas to improve on. Much of this deficiency has to do with habit. Just as spell-checking word processors have weaned many of us from the need to spell correctly, reliance on Excel and other spreadsheet programs has caused many would-be consultants to lose facility with calculations in their heads and with pen and paper.

We'll devote more attention to specific methods to prepare for this later, but in general, the best way to prepare is to accustom yourself to thinking about problems numerically on an ongoing basis. If you are an undergrad, chances are you will consider taking the GMAT at some point; you might consider studying now to gain additional practice on math and logic problems.

## Logic

Fundamentally, it's important that your case analysis make sense to your interviewer. All of us have the capability to reason through problems effectively, but under intense time and pressure, the clarity of logic can break down.

The top mistake consulting case interviewees make is jumping to conclusions. Candidates distracted by an unfamiliar interview format often make faulty assumptions when analyzing problems they would normally dissect with great precision. The cure for this is to maintain a constant awareness of assumptions – state them whenever the need arises, and revisit, modify and reject them as need be to impress your interviewer. Never assume anything. Make sure your statements follow logically.

## Focus

A common pitfall in case interviewing is to get sidetracked on a line of questioning or analysis that is secondary to the key issues that the interviewer has in mind. This happens because candidates get distracted by extraneous facts, or latch onto a well-known framework or tidbit of case information because it provides a quick way to look smart for the interviewer. (Panicked interviewees are especially likely to charge right in and jump at the first thing that looks logical.)

In many respects, focus is what case interviewing is all about. It's a combination of dogged persistence in cutting through unnecessary information, well-honed discipline in sticking to a framework, and listening intently to the interviewer's statements to glean all facts given and pick up on intended or unintended hints. Focus will also lead you away from making too many assumptions based on your own personal experience, since it will lead you to concentrate on the client's situation.

## Business acumen

Business acumen can also be defined as sophistication, or general awareness of business practices. How do you develop your acumen? For starters, read business-related publications, such as *The Wall Street Jounal*. This will help you develop the lingo you need to effectively communicate. Interviewers will notice if you exhibit fluency in a highly valued area of expertise (or at least the appropriate vocabulary). At the same time, it's important to really understand the language you're using. Disconnected buzzwords you picked up through a last-minute scan of the company web site won't fly.

Case frameworks are also a great starting point for building up business acumen. Start to practice by applying the various frameworks in this guide to real-world business problems you work with, read about, or talk about. Through repetition, you will start to see common patterns in how industries are structured, how companies manage their earnings through business cycles, and so on. It takes time to learn things thoroughly, so start now.

# Soft Skills

Consultants are constantly interacting with clients in a wide range of situations with varying comfort levels. Effective consultants must be able to transcend perceived boundaries of age, seniority, experience levels and functional expertise, while finding ways to generate trust and good will among clients who may be inclined to be hostile to interlopers.

## Communication

Clear, articulate, and proactive oral communication is vital to a successful consulting engagement. Having poor communication skills is like having no oil in your car's engine – things break down fast.

It hurts your presentation to use filler words such as "like" and "um" or to appear wobbly under close questioning. Speaking well is a "needed to play" skill for consulting; subtler attention to communication style is needed to win. Your evaluator will be watching closely to see how you mediate your communication styles between formal and informal interactions.

The most obvious area that candidates pay attention to is their formal presentation skills, since consultants often will be presenting recommendations to clients and other team members. However, many candidates neglect to maintain proper transitions from formal delivery of case analysis to the informal interaction with interviewer.

## Composure

All candidates feel nervous the first few times they do a case, and many good consultants will always feel some level of anxiety. In fact, the extra adrenaline that introverted consultants feel from "being on the spot" may ultimately be a differentiator of superior performance down the line.

However, excessive, uncontained jitters can definitely sink your ability to conquer cases and get a job in consulting. The key to overcoming anxiety is to practice the case interviewing style to a point where it no longer feels foreign at all.

If you find yourself freezing when asked a question that temporarily stumps you, take a deep breath and pause. Letting the interviewer know you need a moment to collect your thoughts is a whole lot better than pressing onward and babbling.

## Leadership

Interviewers may adopt exaggerated styles to mimic extremes of client behavior (e.g., the "gruff" client, or the "minimalist communicator" client), but no matter what your interviewer does, they expect you to take charge of the case discussion and exhibit your leadership skills.

As with most aspects of case interviewing, there's more art than science in demonstrating leadership. But there are certain universal best practices. Ask your questions confidently. Seize opportunities to link case discussion to aspects of the interviewers background, or your own. This will help you be deliberate and explicit in showing that you understand the difference between describing your leadership skills and demonstrating them. This is important because, on business school campuses in particular, most candidates' resumes are chock-full of "leadership" roles and titles associated with campus groups. "On-the-job" leadership experience is the "category killer" in this market space, and your perceived value will skyrocket if case interviewers witness through direct interaction how you can take control of a problematic situation.

## Energy

If there is a secret to success at cases, maintaining a high energy level and infusing life into the case discussion just might be it.

Interviewers are keenly aware of the lifestyle demands of consulting and will ruthlessly weed out candidates that lack energy and enthusiasm for tackling case problems. A firm handshake, bright eyes, and a well-rested appearance are the kind of cues interviewers are looking for — "unspoken" messages you send in your body posture and vocal intonations.

It's a bit of a cliché, but you can often sense the energy in the room. Sometimes you leave the interview room knowing you will get the job because you've established a rapport and picked up on many of the interviewer's non-verbal cues. Needless to say, it is extremely difficult to maintain this kind of interaction if you are feeling tired or anxious.

## Final thoughts

Just remember – if you've made it to the case interview, you probably have enough analytical skills to get in the door. Read on for more case strategies to ensure that your talents are appropriately showcased in the interview.

Take advantage of all of Vault's expert insider information and services for consulting careers:

- Vault Guide to the Case Interview – Our best-selling guide has more case frameworks and questions

- Vault Career Guide to Consulting – Detailed insider information on the consulting industry, career paths, and the hiring process

- Vault Consulting Profiles – 50-page profiles on top firms like McKinsey, BCG, Deloitte Consulting, and more

- Vault Case Interview Preparation – One-on-one live phone preparation with a Vault expert

Go to the Vault Consulting Career Channel at http://consulting.vault.com

# How many consulting job boards have you visited lately?

## (Thought so.)

Use the Internet's most targeted job search tools for consulting professionals.

### Vault Consulting Job Board

The most comprehensive and convenient job board for consulting professionals. Target your search by area of consulting, function, and experience level, and find the job openings that you want. No surfing required.

### VaultMatch Resume Database

Vault takes match-making to the next level: post your resume and customize your search by area of consulting, experience and more. We'll match job listings with your interests and criteria and e-mail them directly to your in-box.

VAULT
> the insider career network™

# CASE STRATEGIES AND FRAMEWORKS

# Case Strategies

## Your mission

Whether you are an undergrad anticipating a mixture of market-sizing and business cases, or a second-year MBA student gearing up for a fall recruiting schedule (and potentially facing upwards of 30 cases with five different firms), the objective of case interview preparation remains the same: getting the job.

Business cases are the most rigorous kind of case. Lasting anywhere from 15 minutes to one hour, they are designed to tax your capabilities by engaging your imagination, analytical competency, communication abilities, and relationship-building skills – all simultaneously.

Your objective in this grueling process: use questions to take control of the situation.

## Ask good questions

Cases are designed to be situational – interviewers outline a situation with a business problem, give you a few basic facts, and ask you what you would do in that situation.

It may be helpful to keep in mind that many cases are drawn directly from recent engagement experiences of consultants doing the interviews. Many consultants view the interview process as a valuable tool for "revisiting" a past project, looking at a thorny problem with fresh eyes and potentially gaining the benefit of a bold new approach that you will provide.

When your interviewer opens the case and delivers the first few questions, pause a moment and remind yourself of a key fact: more than likely, this case was based on a real-world business problem for which a client paid something like half a million dollars to a team of consultants to study the problem for at least several weeks. Coming to a conclusive, airtight analysis in 15 minutes is an absurdity. The only thing that matters is establishing the perception of a solid recommendation by building a strong foundation of analysis, primarily with insightful questions.

Simply put, questions are the fundamental building block of effective case interviewing. Questions lay the foundation for analysis, which in turn enables you to summarize and make some basic recommendations.

## Questions set the tone

After the interviewer outlines the problem, you will have a moment to reflect before opening your mouth. Your first response should be a question.

That first question should be "May I take a moment to confirm the details of what you just told me?" After you've made sure you've gotten everything straight, only then should you start asking specific, information-gathering questions.

Questions should be delivered in succinct language, looking directly in the interviewer's eye. After a few questions, you should be able to identify the issues at stake in the case.

## Staying a step ahead

Once you get your bearings, you're ready to pursue a more organized and serious line of questioning.

Try to organize your thoughts into "clusters" of three to four questions. For example, if the case concerns a market entry decision, your first cluster might center on basic characteristics of the market in question, such as market size, competitors and growth trends. If your first cluster of questions sparks any sign of enthusiasm or extra information from your interviewer, you can "explode" that item by asking more specific questions. If not, move on to another element of the framework.

This process may seem straightforward, but under the pressure of an interview you can easily get sidetracked. Your only defense is to make mental and written notes on the question and answer process.

## Dealing with problematic interviewers

The interviewer won't make your job easy. More often than not, your interviewer will use some form of subterfuge to deliberately sidetrack you, either by being cagey, confrontational, or completely passive. A cagey interviewer tries to introduce a new fact or variable every time you map out an assumption. A confrontational interviewer turns the tables on you by constantly asking why you think this fact or that assumption is important. And a passive interviewer surrenders only the minimum information while staring at you blankly.

## Exceed expectations

Like it or not, the clock is your best barometer of case interviewing success and failure. You must either use the clock to your advantage by knowing exactly where you are in the interview, or you will be lost.

Essentially, while the open-ended format of a case does theoretically permit a wide range of paths to a successful recommendation, for practical purposes the "critical path" to a solid recommendation is really quite narrow.

This critical path is determined by the constraints of time and elements for building an argument. It can be conceptualized as a series of four hurdles, each one separating more candidates from success.

# A Step-by-Step Look

What follows is a description of how interviewers evaluate candidates, eliminating a certain percentage from consideration at each interval. All percentages are approximate.

**Hurdle I:   The first two minutes – "When time stands still"**
**(Percentage of candidates dinged at this point = 50 percent)**

First, you must establish the ability to get the basic information you want and need out of the interviewer. You have only two minutes to accomplish this.

Even if your interviewer is pretending to be crusty, rude or non-communicative, keep pressing. Ask your questions and listen carefully to the answers.

At the same time, you need to establish rapport with your interviewer. Rapport can be a bit of appropriate humor, a slight shift in style to show understanding or adjustment. In essence, it's anything that sends the message "I'm with you on this."

It may sound corny, but accommodation is an important consulting skill that keen interviewers will be looking for. You should definitely not be arguing with a client nonstop for a full 15 minutes. A "push-back" exchange may take a minute or two, but normally a client will shift gears into a more manageable mode. "Passive" client types make rapport very difficult to obtain. However, you should make at least one or two attempts at rapport – interviewers may be testing your confidence at taking leadership in building a relationship.

**Hurdle II:   The next three minutes – Establish an analytical approach**
**(Ding rate = 75 percent)**

The next three minutes are for gathering more information. Use a case framework (elaborated in greater detail in the next section), but do so transparently – don't explicitly telegraph your framework to the client. Doing so risks making your analysis seem canned. Frameworks are best used as a kind of mental roadmap, not as the be-all and end-all of case analysis.

The key deliverable in this stage (completing the first five minutes) is to arrive at a definition of the problem. This is a clearer statement of the problem, defined by your investigative questions, and validated by the interviewer.

**Hurdle III: Minutes five to 10 – Moving through the problem**
**(Ding rate = 85 percent)**

As in many aspects of consulting, case interviews are heavily front-loaded; what you do in the beginning has a huge impact on the final outcome.

In minutes five through 10, candidates must be especially conscious of the impact of assumptions. As the old saying goes, "A little knowledge can be a dangerous thing." In other words, don't jump to conclusions too quickly with the facts you've gathered in the first five minutes. To safeguard against faulty or implied assumptions, consider asking rhetorical questions or applying gut checks to your discussion of the problem.

In this stage of the interview, you should be able to explore reasons why the client is having problems and explore possible solutions.

### Hurdle IV: Final five minutes – Reacting, adapting and summarizing concisely
### (Ding rate = 90 percent)

Often, a candidate who's been successful up to this point can expect the client to suddenly change course by introducing a new "critical fact" or key variable. The interviewer's goal is to maximize the difficulty of the interview by forcing you to react to something unexpected. At this stage of the interview, if you've done well before, don't mess up by losing track of your thorough reasoning. Simply incorporate the fact into your logical framework.

If you've made it this far and the client doesn't introduce a change, and you sense you have more time to work with, go back and probe some of your assumptions to search for flaws you missed earlier. Interviewers are always impressed by candidates who keep good mental notes of the entire case.

Always end with a firm, concise summary of your analysis. If your interviewer is even remotely on the fence about your worthiness as a consultant, the confidence you exhibit in your closing argument can tip the balance in your favor. Ask for feedback after you are finished.

# Case Frameworks

## When and how to use case frameworks

When forming an approach to the situational problem in a case interview, it is tremendously helpful to employ a framework to outline your thoughts and structure an answer for your interviewer.

However, be careful. Too often, candidates see frameworks as a magic bullet, believing that simply memorizing them will ensure a fabulous interview. To fully appreciate this pitfall, put yourself in the shoes of a jet-lagged interviewer who's just flown in to deliver the umpteenth case interview on his schedule. The very last thing he wants to hear is a recitation of the Four P's. Have some subtlety. Keep the framework in the back of your mind as a reference point, and think of new ways to spark your discussion.

Don't forget, as a consultant you are getting paid to think. Interviewers will be most impressed with tangible evidence that you are thinking about the problem in a relatively novel and structured way.

## The Three C's

The Three C's is a broad framework of analysis that can be applied to a wide range of business problems for analyzing a company and its environment.

To analyze a company's strategy in relation to its market position, it is necessary to take into account a range of internal and external factors. Customers' needs are the building block – the firm's capacity and cost structure need to be adapted to meet the customer requirements and earn profits. From a competitive standpoint, the capacity and cost structure of the firm should be difficult to imitate in order to sustain the firm's profitability.

### Key questions to ask:

### The Customer

- Who is the customer?
- What is the size of the market? Is the market growing?
- What are the market segments? Which segments are attractive?
- What is the customer's buying decision/value proposition?

### The Company

- What do we do? What differential ability do we have?
- Are we a low-cost or differentiated player?

• What is our organizational structure?

• What is our product? What is its primary value proposition?

### The Competition

• How many competitors are there?

• What is the market structure?

• How does market structure affect pricing?

• Is there excess or a shortage of capacity?

• What is our competitive advantage? Is it sustainable?

In general, the 3 C's framework should answer the question: What is our firm's chance for profitability in this industry? The framework is usually best for market entry, profitability, and open-ended types of cases.

## The Four P's

Most useful for cases that focus on marketing issues, such as:

• New product strategy

• Development of new markets for old products

• Programs to increase market share

The Four P's of marketing is a versatile framework that will come in very handy in many cases. Marketing is a central element of business strategy, so the Four P's are a particularly useful.

### Price

The price a firm sets for its product or service can be a strategic advantage. For example, it can be predatory (set very low to undercut the competition), or it can be set slightly above market average to convey a "premium" image. Consider how pricing is being used in the context of the case presented to you.

### Product

The product or service may provide a strategic advantage if it is the only product or service that satisfies a particular intersection of customer needs. Or it may simply be an extension of already existing products, and therefore not much of a benefit. Try to tease out the value of the product in the marketplace, based on the case details you have been given.

### Position/Place

The physical location of a product or service can provide an advantage if it is superior to its competition, if it is easier or more convenient for people to consume, or if it makes the consumer more aware of the product or service over its competition. In the context of a business case, you may want to determine the placement of the product or service compared to its competition.

### Promotion

With so much noise in today's consumer (and business to business) marketplace, it is difficult for any one product or service to stand out in a category. Promotional activity (including advertising, discounting to consumers and suppliers, celebrity appearances, etc.) can be used to create or maintain consumer awareness, open new markets, or target a specific competitor. You may want to suggest a promotional strategy in the context of the case you are presented.

## Porter's Five Forces

Porter's Five Forces, as presented by Harvard Business School professor Michael Porter in the 1980s, is a classic framework for industry analysis. In practice, managers often use this framework to assess the attractiveness of their current industry as well as potential markets they want to enter. It offers a snapshot of the state of an industry and is a useful place to start any case with an industry attractiveness component.

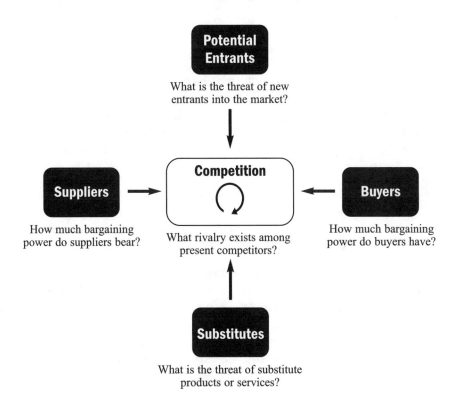

Take, for example, entry into the copy store market (like Kinko's). How attractive is the copy store market?

**Potential entrants:** What is the threat of new entrants into the market? Copy stores are not very expensive to open – you can conceivably open a copy store with one copier and one employee. Therefore, barriers to entry are low, so there's a high risk of potential new entrants.

**Buyer power:** How much bargaining power do buyers have? Copy store customers are relatively price sensitive. Between the choice of a copy store that charges $.05 a copy and a store that charges $.06 a copy, buyers will usually head for the cheaper store. Because copy stores are common, buyers have the leverage to bargain with copy store owners on large print jobs or can threaten to take their business elsewhere. The only mitigating factors are location and hours. On the other hand, price is not the only factor. Copy stores that are willing to stay open 24 hours may be able to charge a premium, and customers may simply patronize the copy store closest to them if other locations are relatively inconvenient.

**Supplier power:** How much bargaining power do suppliers have? While paper prices may be on the rise, copier prices continue to fall. The skill level employees need to operate a copy shop (for basic services, like copying, collating, and so on) are relatively low as well, meaning that employees will have little bargaining power. Suppliers in this situation have low bargaining power.

**Threat of substitutes:** What is the risk of substitution? For basic copying jobs, more people now possess color printers at home. Additionally, fax machines have the capability to perform copy functions as well. Large companies will normally have their own copying facilities. The Internet is a potential threat to copy stores as well, because some documents that formerly would be distributed in hard copy will now be posted on the Web or sent through e-mail. However, for the time being, there is still relatively strong demand for copy store services.

**Competition:** Competition within the industry appears to be intense. Stores often compete on price and are willing to "underbid" one another to win printing contracts. Stores continue to add new features to compete as well, such as expanding hours to 24-hour service and offering free delivery.

From this analysis, you can ascertain that copy stores are something of a commodity market. Consumers are very price-sensitive; copy stores are inexpensive to set up; and the market is relatively easy for competitors to enter. Advances in technology may reduce the size of the copy store market. Value-added services, such as late hours, convenient locations, or additional services (such as creating calendars or stickers) may help copy stores differentiate themselves. But overall, the copy store industry does not appear to be an attractive one.

## PIE - The next generation of Porter's Five Forces

In their 2001 text *Strategic Management*, Garth Saloner, Andrea Shepard and Joel Podolny refined the Five Forces Model and introduced the concept of Potential Industry Earnings (PIE) to the analysis to reflect a firm's ability to enjoy its share of the industry profits. This addition is helpful in assessing the share of profits that the group of incumbent firms retains from the total industry value.

### PIE = Total value added by the industry – Total cost to produce the goods

Some industries like solar power have a high total value for the consumer, but also an extremely high opportunity cost to produce goods. Photoelectric cells have high research and development as well as production and installation costs and therefore low PIE. The diamond industry and the designer clothing industry have significant PIE, since they are able to create significant value, as shown in the prices customers are willing to pay, at a low opportunity cost.

### Potential entrants

Barriers to entry such as high capital costs, proprietary technology or patents, and scale and branding of existing competitors prevent the erosion of profits by new competitors. For example, industries with low cost of entry and undifferentiated products, such as ocean fisheries that only require a boat and a small crew, means that incumbent fisheries are not likely to capture a large share of profits unless they can create some type of barrier to new entrants such as scale or branding or some sort.

### Supplier power

Suppliers are providers of the inputs to the industry being evaluated. This may include labor unions and raw materials providers, among others. Concentration of suppliers and internal competition among them determines how much leverage suppliers can have over the industry and how much of the PIE they can capture. For example, the diamond wholesaling industry depends on diamond mining and purchasing cartels to provide its inputs. A few companies control a majority of diamonds sold on the market. De Beers, one of the largest players, has pushed towards a vertical structure in which they take the diamonds to market themselves, cutting out the middle layers. The concentration of the suppliers and their power to cut off supply gives them the ability to take PIE from the diamond wholesalers and makes that industry much less attractive. to a potential new competitor

## Buyer power

Buyers are the outlets for the products of the industry. The power of the buyers can take away significant PIE from incumbents. Concentration among buyers and their internal competitiveness are both determinants of buyer strength. For example, Wal-Mart and Target are very large customers of many consumer goods companies. They have a great deal of leverage over small and medium suppliers simply because of their size and scale. Not making it onto Wal-Mart's shelves can mean the difference between a successful and an unsuccessful product launch. Knowing this, Wal-Mart buyers can leverage their strength into lower wholesale prices. As a result, smaller manufacturers are not able to capture a large portion of the PIE because there are substitutes for their products.

## Substitutes

The availability of acceptable substitutes can cause buyers and end customers to bypass the industry products completely and lower the size of the overall PIE. For example, at one time there were few substitutes to public pay phones; today, however, cellular phones and calling cards are considered acceptable substitutes.

## Internal competition

Internal competition is usually less intense in industries in which a large portionof the market is split among one or a few large players and products are somewhat differentiated. However, these rules of thumb are not always true. For example, high concentration OPEC, the cartel of oil rich countries, has recently been able to discipline the market and raise oil prices by limiting output, but even it has been the victim of the freerider problem with some countries secretly overselling their quota to maximize profits over the good of the whole.

## Value disciplines

In 1992, the concept of value disciplines were introduced to explain how some companies are able to achieve and maintain market leadership despite being in competitive industries. By identifying what is most important for an industry and its customers, you can make specific recommendations about the direction a company should go.

Companies who surpass competitors in one of the three value disciplines can achieve success. The three value disciplines include:

## 1. Operational excellence

Companies who employ this value discipline focus on efficient internal operations as the means to market leadership. For example, Toyota has used its manufacturing process leadership to produce high quality cars at a relatively low cost.

## 2. Customer intimacy

Companies who pursue customer intimacy focus on understanding their customers pain points and anticipating their needs. Amazon.com is one example of a company that creates a "market segment of one" for its customers by extensive recommendations and tailored marketing.

## 3. Product leadership

Companies that exhibit product leadership are innovators, well ahead of the technology and product curves. For example, Nokia continuously pursues leading technology and product design to meet its customer needs.

# SWOT Analysis

Strength-Weakness/Opportunity-Threat Analysis is another general tool, similar to the 3C's, for use in analyzing a company within its business environment.

The value of SWOT is in assessing how a company can use its superior capabilities to capitalize on new opportunities, while mitigating risks due to weaknesses and threats.

| Strengths/Weaknesses | Used to analyze the capabilities of the company |
|---|---|
| Opportunities/Threats | Used to evaluate the company's environment |

Let's take the example of Calson Wagonlit Travel, one of the largest travel planning services in the U.S. It specializes in business travel, with some leisure components, and is often the in-house travel agency for major corporations.

## Strengths

What are the company's strengths? Carlson Wagonlit has a major installed base within the corporations of the world. Its strong brand, formidable size and multinational presence are all strengths. Also, it has institutional capabilities and a network of knowledgeable employees to deliver its product.

## Weaknesses

What are the company's weaknesses? Carlson Wagonlit's success fluctuates with the economy. Its business model is dependent on airline ticket commissions, which have been decreasing in recent years. Also the company has major corporate customers who are seeking to lower their travel expenses. This can exert a great deal of price pressure on Carlson's other value-added services.

## Opportunities

What opportunities does the company have? The installed base and strong brand can be leveraged into other value-added services for business and leisure travel. Additionally, it can refocus on more high-priced niche travel planning services for which users will pay a premium.

## Threats

What market threats does the company face? With the availability of travel planning on the Web, corporate employees can now find their own fares and schedules without the assistance of Carlson Wagonlit. Additionally, some companies have been experimenting with allowing employees to retain a portion of the savings for booking lower-priced, restricted travel tickets. This trend will encourage end customers to bypass corporate travel agencies and seek out the best travel plans on their own.

The SWOT framework is simple to employ and useful in trying to understand the position of a company. Based on the above SWOT analysis, Carlson Wagonlit has many important strengths that it can leverage going forward, but also faces a changing industry and revenue model. Its ability to evolve in light of these threats will be key to its long-term success.

## The Seven S Framework

The Seven S Framework is a useful framework for analyzing the "internals" of a company (i.e., to determine the sources of competitive advantage for a company). The framework is a McKinsey favorite. In this model, all seven "S's" are needed to form a "network" that reinforces and sustains competitive advantage. The logic is that competitors may find it possible to duplicate any one of the "S" attributes, but it will be nearly impossible to copy the complex web of interrelationships between them.

| Hardware | Software |
|---|---|
| • Strategy<br>• Structure<br>• Systems | • Staff<br>• Skills<br>• Style<br>• Shared Values |

**Has your job offer been delayed – or rescinded? Are you trying to get into the consulting job market or trying to move to another firm? Then you know it's tough – and that you need every advantage you can get.**

We know the consulting industry. We've got experts and practicing consultants ready to review your resume and give you the competitive advantage you need.

## Consulting Resume Writing and Resume Reviews

• Have your resume written from scratch or reviewed by an expert that knows the consulting industry and has seen hundreds if not thousands of consultants' resumes.

• For resume writing, start with an e-mailed history and 1- to 2-hour phone discussion. Our experts will write a first draft, and deliver a final draft after feedback and discussion.

• For resume reviews, get an in-depth critique and rewrite within TWO BUSINESS DAYS.

## Consulting Career Coaching

• Want to know what it takes to get into consulting from school or another career?

• Have a deferred acceptance and want to know where to go from here?

• Looking to switch from one consulting firm to another?

• Is the travel wearing you out and you're looking to see how else your consulting skills can be put to use?

## For more information go to http://consulting.vault.com

**VAULT**
> the insider career network™

# SAMPLE CASES

# Case 1: Pricing Rooms

> **Your client is a mid-sized hotel chain. How would you develop a pricing strategy for the client?**

*While price is one of the elements of the Four P's framework (product, place, promotion and price) the Three C's framework is probably the best tool to apply to this question.*

*The most logical starting point is to ask questions about the product or service.*

**You:** What kind of customers does the hotel cater to? Vacationers or business travelers? Are the hotel's offerings positioned for a low budget, mid-range, or upscale clientele?

*Interviewer:* The hotel chain targets vacationers and business travelers, depending on the location.

**You:** What do customers say about the hotel?

*Interviewer:* A customer satisfaction survey indicates its service levels fall in the middle of the market.

> *Here's an opportunity to demonstrate some knowledge of pricing strategies. Since the hotel targets different guest segments at different locations, the client may want to consider a differentiated pricing policy. Based on your experience, you would like to assume that business travelers are generally less price-sensitive than vacationers. But better let your interviewer confirm that for you.*

**You:** How do customers make their purchase decisions?

*Interviewer:* The customer survey of business and vacation travelers revealed that business travelers value service and convenience highest within a standard price range, while vacation travelers are less elastic with regard to price.

> *File this away for future use. You might suggest developing a differentiated pricing scheme that offers discounts to guests who stay over Saturday nights or who stay longer than three nights (these are likely to be vacation travelers). At this point you have explored the segmenting and positioning strategy of the hotel chain, the first of the Three Cs. The next step is to identify the next best option for the customer: the direct competitors and sometimes-competitors.*

*You:*           Who are the main competitors of my client?

*Interviewer:*  Each hotel site has a number of competitors within close proximity. These hotels serve the same market segment.

> ***Be that as it may, there has to be some differentiation. Make it your job to find out just how your client stacks up against competitors.***

*You:*           How does my client compare to competitors in terms of rooms, price, amenities and location?

                [Note that in a real case, this might take several questions.]

*Interviewer:*  The client's rooms and amenities are slightly nicer than those of its competitors, featuring amenities like Internet connections and in-room coffee makers, while service levels and location are comparable or slightly inferior to those of competitors. Competitors' prices for weeknights range from $110 to $140 per night and from $80 to $95 per night on the weekends.

> ***Is there any room for expansion? You had better figure this out.***

*You:*           How close to capacity is the market? Are there enough rooms to meet demand?

*Interviewer:*  Yes. Except for periodically high demand in some locations, there is enough capacity. In some locations, there is overcapacity.

> ***Okay, at this point the interviewer is giving out some hard data, and enough questions have been asked to start your analysis. Here's how you might phrase your analysis and suggestions.***

*You:*           The hotel business and airline business have some similarities. Both have high fixed costs. The hotel will be there whether or not anyone stays in it. On the one hand, the hotel needs to fill as many rooms as possible. On the other hand, a price war can soon cause profits to fall below fixed costs. Simply undercutting all competitors on price doesn't make sense.

           At the same time, because our hotels are not clearly superior to our competitors, raising prices above those of competitors would not make sense either.

           First of all, I would recommend taking a two-pronged approach to pricing. Pricing for business travelers, i.e., travelers during the week, should be higher than for weekend travelers. The firm should also consider an even lower "budget" level to fill rooms. This could be through special offers released via the Internet to frequent customers, and/or signing up with services like Priceline to offload unused rooms.

Business travelers, in general, are much more sensitive to factors like service and location, while leisure travelers typically focus more on price and location. Since we will expect that business travelers will pay more, I would focus on improving our service to business travelers. Perhaps a shuttle service or other courtesy service might offset any location disadvantages. As for leisure travelers, we should consider promoting any of our hotels that are in especially desirable tourist areas, like New York City or New Orleans.

# Case 2: Wireless Without Profit

> **Your client is a manufacturer of handheld wireless devices. The client is gaining market share but seeing declining profits. Why? What should it do?**

*Revenue for a manufacturer is a function of sales volume multiplied by sales price. The interviewer has already tipped us off that sales volume is increasing (that is, market share is going up). Logically, in order for profits to fall in this situation, prices must be declining or costs must be going up. The other possibility is a combination of these two situations.*

*Interviewer:* Our client has been dropping prices, and expenses have been trending higher.

> ***Zeroing in on the client's pricing is probably the best place to dig in for further questioning. Pricing is a conscious decision by the client, and it is possible that the client has decreased its prices intentionally to gain market share. Or the client might have been forced to drop prices in order to follow competitors' lead.***

*You:* What is the client's pricing strategy?

*Interviewer:* Our client's pricing strategy is based on matching the low-price leader in the market.

> ***Now you are starting to get valuable information. If companies in this market are lowering prices, there could either be an oversupply of handheld wireless devices, or certain competitors might have lower cost structures which enable them to earn a profit at a lower price. Certainly it would be helpful to develop a comparison of the cost structure between our client and its competitors.***

*You:* How many low-price leaders are there?

*Interviewer:* As it turns out, several new entrants to the market have successfully established positions as low cost producers.

> ***This is where the client's broader strategic objectives come to bear. To deal with this problem, the client has two basic choices: it can either attempt to reduce costs in order to be competitive with the new entrants, or it can focus attention on strengthening its presence in customer segments in which it has stronger product differentiation. Of course, to determine either, you first need a clear idea of what the client does!***

*You:*         What does our client make?

*Interviewer:*  The client makes wireless-enabled tablets, much like the Palm Pilot.

*You:*         How are these products distributed?

*Interviewer:*  The client sells most of this hardware to large corporate buyers through a direct sales force. About 20 percent is sold to smaller companies and individuals.

*While you are not overly familiar with this type of product and its applications, a possible method for segmenting the market is to consider potential purchasers:*

*1) Fortune 500 corporations (aka large corporate buyers)*
*2) Small and mid-sized companies*
*3) Sole proprietors and individual consumers*

*Clearly, these segments exhibit diverse buying behavior, based on different needs and budget resources. It's time to state an assumption and see if it flies with the interviewer.*

*You:*         I assume that our large corporate buyers value strong after-sales support, are willing to pay for the most advanced machines, and buy larger volume orders with less price sensitivity.

*Interviewer:*  That's true.

*The Fortune 500 corporate market is very desirable, and probably the strongest long-term position for competitors in this market. Therefore, it's important to find out how the client's product/service bundle matches the needs of this segment, and what the new competitors are offering.*

*You:*         What is our after-sales support like? And can you discuss our R&D (that's research and development) capabilities?

*Interviewer:*  Yes, the client is noted for a very strong service department and its R&D capabilities consistently generate new features. The new low-price entrants have mimicked most of the technology features of our client's product, but the competitors' products are marketed through retail channels where little after-sales support is provided.

*This is enough information to reach a tentative conclusion. The client seems to be pricing its products incorrectly. While it is matching the new entrants' aggressive prices, the product/service mix is superior to the low-price competitors' offerings.*

**You:**    Market share is probably increasing simply because the price drop increases the value proposition to customers because the firm offers a superior product for the same price as its competitors. The fact that profitability is declining indicates that demand is fairly inelastic, since the increase in sales is not making up for the decreased margins. Therefore, our client may want to raise its prices and focus on maintaining a strong niche with the large corporate buyer market.

*You're not done yet – don't forget the expense side of the problem (remember back to the original question?). It's important to determine why expenses are increasing.*

**You:**    Have R&D costs increased as a result of the competition?

*Interviewer:*    No, they have remained stable.

**You:**    Has the company opened up any new plants to supply the increased demand?

*Interviewer:*    No, our current plants are not yet at capacity and are functional, modern facilities. Our client's costs have increased because management has aggressively added new sales and support people to keep pace with growth.

**You:**    Increased sales and support staff gives the company advantages in servicing its primary market segment, but there is a risk in raising cost structure too high, to a point where end-users can't justify the premium pricing. It would be worthwhile for the client to perform a study on the size and activities of its sales staff, comparing costs to benchmarks from within its industry and other industries.

# Case 3: Sell That Satellite!

> Your client is an entrepreneur in partnership with three private investors. The client purchased a satellite from a now-bankrupt global telecommunications company. A large company has offered the client $9 million for the satellite, and the partnership has requested your advice in deciding whether to accept this offer.

*Don't be fooled – while the $9 million number seems convenient, the value of the satellite is best determined through assessment of "forward looking" cash flows. You need to determine what kind of cash flows the asset can generate at its most productive use, and discount the cash flows at an appropriate discount rate to calculate the net present value.*

*The first step is obviously to investigate what the productive uses for the asset might be. It's common knowledge that satellites can be used for transmission of data such as telephone, TV, or computer data. Lesser-known applications include espionage (e.g., taking photographs of the planet) or for scientific research.*

**You:** What is this satellite for?

*Interviewer:* The satellite was designed specifically for the global telecom company to serve as a conduit for data transmission. The original owner used it to transmit telephone services.

**You:** I would suggest assessing the demand of satellite-based telephone data transmission as opposed to land and wire-based.

*Interviewer:* The partnership has already determined that satellite data transmission for telephones is superior to land and wire-based data transmission.

*Something doesn't sound right, however. If satellite data transmission for telephones is so desirable, why did the owner of the satellite go bankrupt? Well, why not ask?*

**You:** Why is the satellite for sale?

*Interviewer:* As I said, because the company that owned the satellite went bankrupt.

*Don't be put off. Press your questioning.*

*You:*         Why did the company go bankrupt?

*Interviewer:*   There is a problem with the orbit of the satellite. As a consequence of the orbit, the satellite can only send and receive signals during eight hours of the day, from 6:00 pm until about 2:00 am.

*This is a very serious flaw. Reliability is a major factor in providing a service like data transmission. One option is to launch another satellite, or even two satellites, with different orbits to complete the coverage area. Naturally, the cost of launching one or two satellites would need to be rationalized against the cost of launching one new satellite capable of 24-hour service.*

*You:*         How much does it cost to launch a satellite?

*Interviewer:*   The cost of launching a 24-hour satellite is $25 million. The cost of launching one 8-hour satellite is $12 million.

*You pause a moment to review the facts. Pushing aside the $9 million reference point, you realize that the old satellite needs to be valued in the new context. It would cost $36 million to assemble the same coverage from three 8-hour satellites, vs. $25 Million for the 24-hour coverage satellite. Based on comparison to the $25 million satellite, your old satellite would only be worth $1 million (two new 8-hour satellites at $12 million each = $24 million, subtracted from $25 million, = $1 million).*

*Assuming the information is accurate, at this point two major possibilities exist. First, the $9 million offer could be from a naïve buyer (assuming the real value of the satellite is $1 million), in which case the profit-maximizing entrepreneur would want to sell the asset.*

*Secondly, there could be another use for the satellite beyond data transmission that generates enough cash flow to justify a higher valuation.*

*You'd better get more information about the buyer.*

*You:*         Who is the potential buyer?

*Interviewer:*   The buyer is a data storage firm that services the financial industry.

Building on your hypothesis of alternative uses, you note that 8-hour coverage is less essential to other types of information transmission – transmission of computer data, for example. The satellite could potentially serve as an outsourced transmission service for companies that need to back up data at regular intervals in a 24-hour period.

*You:*     It sounds to me like the satellite is not worth $9 million as a telephone satellite. The question is whether it is worth $9 million as a financial data satellite. I would carefully research this market before deciding whether or not to accept this offer, including determining how many other similar satellites are up for sale.

# Case 4:  Rehabilitation Center

> Your client is a not-for-profit firm.  It owns and manages a national chain of rehabilitation centers that provide health care services to the elderly.  The last two years have seen a decline in profitability in the existing business, and the firm is seeking new growth opportunities to offset this trend.

*Since profits are declining, it is worthwhile to reevaluate?  Ask.*

**You:**  What is our current business model?

**Interviewer:**  The current model often includes overnight stays of one or several days.

**You:**  So it sounds like our patients aren't suffering any severe illnesses.

**Interviewer:**  No, our patients do not suffer from life-threatening illnesses.  They are patients who need rehabilitation.  We also get patients who have been discharged from the hospital but need more nurturing and care than their families can give them.

*You should determine what's driving up costs.*

**You:**  Tell me about the firm's expenses

**Interviewer:**  The cost of providing overnight accommodation is significant in the current business model.

*Day care is an increasingly important part of elder care.  Investigate this possibility. This would prevent the expenses of overnight stays.*

**You:**  Have you considered converting the chain to day care, as opposed to long-term stays?

**Interviewer:**  In fact, the client has been considering such a change.  How would you advise your client to proceed?  What are the issues that they must consider?

*Good for you.  The interviewer has been driving towards this point.  But first, make sure that you understand what you're supposed to accomplish.*

*You:*     I would like to clarify the primary objective of the firm. Shall I assume that profitability is a key objective, even though the firm is a not-for-profit?

*This is important to clarify upfront, since the interviewer mentions that this is a not-for-profit firm. It could be that the organization has other objectives, such as increasing the number of clients served.*

*Interviewer:* Yes, focus on reversing the declining profit trend.

*You:*     Is the firm considering changing the business model in all, or some of, its existing rehab centers? Or is the proposed model a new venture?

*Interviewer:* I'm glad you asked that. The company does not intend to transform existing rehab centers. Rather it intends to establish new centers using the proposed day care model.

*This is an important indication that the interviewer wants you to evaluate the feasibility of a new model. It implies that you don't need to evaluate the existing model, but structure the discussion towards the new model.*

*You:*     Well, here is how I would like to structure the discussion going forward. First, I would like to assess the market opportunity and determine the viability of this new business model. Second, if the new venture is found to be feasible, I would like to assess the firm's capabilities and resources in proceeding with it. Finally, I will make a recommendation based on the facts and the discussion we will have.

*It's useful to frame the structure of the discussion upfront. Take a few moments before you do this, and make sure you've considered, at least broadly, all the issues you want to address. This exercise also gives you an agenda for the case analysis and demonstrates clear thinking. Once you have done this, you can begin to ask questions about each agenda item.*

*Interviewer:* Sounds good.

*You:*     Could you please tell me a little about the rehab center industry, and especially the markets in which our client operates?

*Interviewer:* The elderly clientele generally uses rehab centers as they recover from an illness. Our client is one of the largest firms in the industry. The competition essentially follows a similar business model, providing health care and nursing services, including overnight stays. The average rehab center has 100 beds.

*The interviewer is providing you with some information, but is probably holding some back as well. Use this as a clue to keep asking questions until you feel you have enough information to make hypotheses.*

*You:* What are the revenue streams?

*In a business, the "topline," or where the revenues come from, is a very important issue. The answer to this will put you at ease that the company has thought about this issue and has identified a customer base, which you should explore next.*

*Interviewer:* Revenue streams accrue primarily from medical services provided.

*You:* Who pays – the patient or insurance?

*Interviewer:* Payments are made by third party payors, such as Medicare, PPOs and so on.

*You:* What is the typical consumer profile?

*Interviewer:* Why don't you take a crack at constructing a consumer profile for me?

*Interviewers often answer questions with questions. Don't be alarmed. Often they're saying that you have enough information to hazard a guess yourself.*

*You:* I would expect that typical users of these centers fit the following profile: over 60 years old, recently undergone some major surgery or other medical procedure, typically with a medium to long post-surgical recovery period during which some medical oversight is necessary.

*Interviewer:* That's about right.

*You:* What attempts have been made by our client to assess the financial feasibility of a day care rehab center?

*After you've determined that there are customers who would find this service useful, and that revenues can be realized, the next step is to consider the costs. The financial feasibility brings together both revenues and costs and is a good starting point to do the numbers.*

*Interviewer:*     A pilot center was, in fact, constructed in a suburb of Chicago. Here are the results from that study:

| Payor Type | % Total Revenue | Profit Margin |
|---|---|---|
| A – Medicare | 20% | 0% |
| B – PPO | 60% | 60% |
| C – Medicaid | 10% | 0% |
| D – Others/Charity | 10% | 20% |

*You see the numbers, but you want to make sure that you can base your judgments on them, and that the numbers will not change if the scale changes. Since these are the results of a pilot center, you really don't know what an entire business built on this concept will look like. You must clarify these doubts.*

*You:*     Well, it's certainly heartening to see that the largest segment (the PPO) has the highest profit margin. I would, however, like to ascertain if these numbers are representative of a potential national, or even regional, rollout of day care rehab centers. In other words, is there any reason to believe that profit margins might increase as a result of scale? Or that the relative sizes of the four segments at the pilot might differ from the market as a whole?

*Interviewer:*     No, and no to both your questions. Our client has reason to believe that the segment sizes and profitability at the pilot is accurate of the business at large. At this point, could you sum up for me the various issues that our client must consider to assess the market opportunity?

*This is the interviewer asking for your hypothesis. It's a signal that he feels that you now have enough information to construct a hypothesis. Take a few minutes to gather your thoughts, revisit the facts you have gathered and then answer his question.*

*You:*     Yes, certainly. The market opportunity assessment must consider all of the following factors.

**Target payor type segment:**     Only two payor segments are profitable:  PPO and Others – it is these that the client must target. What is the total size, and growth rates, of these segments?

**Customer segment:** The client must profile the typical consumers who would benefit from day care rehab centers. The advertising and promotion strategy would depend on this.

**Location:** Choice of location for individual centers must be made based on concentrations of the targeted customer segment (downtown vs. suburbs etc.). In addition, it is important to look at various regions to determine a national rollout sequence.

**Cannibalization:** There is a possibility that some of the existing business might decline as a result of this new day care product offering; it is important to consider this.

**Competition:** It would be useful to assess competitive responses to this new venture.

**Financials:** Finally, all of the above must be consolidated into a forecast of financial feasibility, in order to determine the attractiveness of this new venture.

*Interviewer:* Good. What else would you consider?

*It is not enough to determine feasibility of a project; it's important to determine if an organization has the resources to capitalize on it. This is a good choice for what you should explore next.*

*You:* Assuming that the financial assessment of the venture is positive, I would also like to consider our client's internal resources and capabilities to proceed with it, including financing options.

*Interviewer:* Actually, the firm is considering various options, such as spinning it off as a new business and obtaining venture capital funding. What do you think of this plan?

*You:* If the primary constraint is financing, a spin-off may be appropriate. However, the disadvantages of a spin-off would be substantial. The new company may not have access to the current management and its experience in the industry. There may be other synergies in purchasing, operations, training, or marketing that may not be available to the new company. On the other hand, there are benefits of a spin-off as well: management's attention would not be diluted, and the risks of a new venture would not impact the existing business.

*Interviewer:* What would you recommend?

*Don't be afraid to make a stand. Weigh the options and present an argument in favor of your recommendation. Often there is no right answer.*

**You:** Our client should make the decision based on its assessment of the advantages and disadvantages of a spin-off versus an internal division. I imagine that keeping the project in-house might actually be more valuable, given the synergistic benefits.

*Interviewer:* Assuming the outcome of the financial feasibility forecast was positive, what would your final recommendation be?

**You:** I would recommend that our client proceed with the day care rehab centers, beginning with those locations that have the highest concentrations of our target customer group, and lowest current penetration. In addition, the firm should fully exploit its experience in this industry and leverage all possible synergistic benefits. Finally, I would recommend that the project be carried out in-house, rather than being spun off, provided it is possible to raise the necessary funding at reasonable rates.

---

### Vault Bonus Case Analysis

This case is a new business feasibility analysis. As a consultant, you will have to assess the following factors:

**Market opportunity:** Assess the opportunity in this new segment.

**Financial feasibility:** Analyze the financials that the client has constructed, and pay special attention to the assumptions on which the model is based.

**Resources and capabilities:** Discuss with the client if it has the human resources and organizational resources to pursue this project. Will it take too much management attention? Is it the best investment of resources this company has, given other opportunities?

**The financing decision:** Finally, if the company should decide to pursue this opportunity, you may have to evaluate the different sources of financing available.

---

# Case 5: E-Voting

> You have been staffed on a consulting team that has been selected to advise a southern state in the United States on the issue of electronic voting. The state government has been toying with the idea of using electronic voting to increase voter turnout. However, it also wants to do this at a reasonable cost.

*How would you frame this problem? What are the various issues you would like to analyze?*

**You:**       Could you explain electronic voting to me?

> *Don't hesitate to ask for clarifications or definitions once you've been presented the case, or at any time during the discussion. It's essential that you share the interviewer's understanding of the key terms.*

*Interviewer:*   E-voting, as defined by your client, is any system that captures votes electronically, rather than by a manual ballot.

> *The interviewer defines e-voting quite broadly; there's no harm in asking a second clarifying question, this time using examples, so there's absolutely no doubt that you're both on the same page.*

**You:**       So, e-voting might refer to a PC in a voting booth, or to a web site that can be accessed by a voter over the Internet?

*Interviewer:*   Precisely.

> *After you've clarified the situation, it's advisable to set the agenda for the discussion, as early on in the discussion as possible. This is what you should do next:*

**You:**       I'd like to structure this analysis by first understanding the impediments to increasing voter turnout. I'd then like to analyze how e-voting might aid in this effort and the pros and cons of using e-voting, specifically the costs and benefits. This is how I would frame the problem.

*Interviewer:*   OK.

> *Of course, simply having a computer in a regular voting booth most likely is not going to make much of an impact on voter turnout (though it might improve voting*

*accuracy). If you're going to assume that for the purposes of this study e-voting applies only to the ability to vote via computer at many locations, then say so.*

**You:**  I am going to assume that we will study voting by computers outside the voting booth.

*Interviewer:*  That's fine.

*Now go ahead and make specific inquiries. In this case, the first issue is: who's not voting, and will e-voting rectify the situation?*

**You:**  Has our client observed any patterns in voter turnout? Are specific populations less likely than others to vote? What, if any, are the demographic variables which have a bearing on voter turnout?

*Interviewer:*  These are all good questions. There has been a preliminary analysis of citizens who do not participate in elections. But since all voting has been manual, there is a scarcity of data. Our client has made certain educated guesses on the groups of people who they would like to target, but is hoping for us to push the thinking forward in this area. How would you do this?

*The interviewer doesn't really give you any information to work with here, and instead asks you to speculate on the reasons why voters might not vote. This is easier than it seems. You can do this in several ways. You can list all the reasons why they might not vote; or you can classify non-voters into a couple of different groups. Let's use the second approach. (If you used the first approach, you would need to list reasons such as lack of time, disinterest, lack of mobility, etc.)*

**You:**  I would separate the chronic non-voters from the occasional non-voters. I would like to focus on the former group. The latter group might remain absent for unavoidable reasons such as illness or travel.

*Interviewer:*  Sounds reasonable.

*Another way in which you can classify non-voters is by demographic variables such as age, income or sex. Remember that you're doing this so you can match the demographics of desired users with the demographics of non-voters. If these two groups match, then e-voting over the Internet might be a good way to increase turnout.*

**You:**  I don't have adequate information to identify specific demographic variables, but this is what I would like to identify: What are the demographics of chronic non-voters?

*Interviewer:* The client has identified two such groups of "chronic non-voters": senior citizens, age 65 and over; and young professionals between the ages of 25 and 35.

**You:** That is very helpful. I would now like to understand if e-voting will help to increase participation rates in these two groups. In order to do this, it would be helpful to understand why these two groups have lower participation rates to begin with. My hypothesis is that mobility may be a problem with the senior citizens, while busy schedules might avert the young professionals from voting.

If this were the case, e-voting would address both these problems. Participating from a remote location might be possible with Internet voting. This should increase senior citizen participation. In addition, remote e-voting is less time consuming than voting in physical booths. This should increase professional participation rates.

*Interviewer:* But e-voting is not without its disadvantages. What are some of these?

**You:** There are at least three major disadvantages. First, security remains problematic. While electronic signatures are now legal, confirming identity remains a problem on the Internet. Second, there is the issue of connectivity and access. While the young professionals probably have a higher Internet penetration, the senior citizens may not all have access. Third, there remains the issue of benefit versus cost.

*Interviewer:* What can our client do to address these problems?

*Internet security is a huge issue, and you know that governments and various private organizations are looking at it. You're not sure what a state or city government can do to add to this discussion.*

**You:** There is little our client can do unilaterally to tackle the issue of security. This is a much larger problem that needs to be resolved. I would recommend that our client avoid taking a seat at this table, but follow the progress closely. I would expect that at some point reasonable and cost-effective solutions to this problem would be invented.

*Interviewer:* And access?

*Access is a big problem. Not everybody has a computer. You realize that if non-voters have access to the Internet, then it's not a problem. If they don't, then it's a problem, so try to make some suggestions of getting around it.*

**You:**　　　Access is a problem. Our client has to determine if a significant proportion of non-voters has access to the Internet or not. If so, then it would make targeting them to participate in elections much easier. If not, then there might be ways in which increasing access might be possible – for instance, using school and library computers to allow individuals to vote.

This actually has to deal with another issue. I see e-voting as a solution to increasing turnout. If specific demographic groups have been identified, marketing and advertising campaigns can target these groups, urging them to participate.

My guess would be that voters in the 25 to 35 demographic would be more likely to vote as a result of this initiative, as the constraint on their voting is most likely time and not mobility.

*Interviewer:*　　And benefit versus cost?

*Here's where you have to consider if the additional cost of providing e-voting is justified by the increase in the number of voters the system attracts.*

**You:**　　　The cost of an e-voting system should be relatively simple to estimate. The major components would be the cost of technology and administration. A revealing cost metric might be the expense incurred per additional voter. The state also has to consider if it has the budget to fund this project, or if it can free the funds required and create a budget for it. There might also be some sort of federal initiative to increase voter turnout, which could help fund this project.

The benefits are harder to measure. I would expect that as participation rates increase, marginal benefits of inclusion fall. In other words, a state beginning with a lower participation rate would have a higher marginal benefit from this system than a state with a higher rate.

## Vault Bonus Case Analysis

This case tests case skills in a non-business environment. The interviewer sets up the case as an evaluation of a particular technology. It is important to appraise possible technology solutions in light of the goal, which in this case is to increase voter participation rates. Probe into the underlying factors that influence participation and evaluate the appropriateness of the proposed technology solution in this context.

# Case 6: Al's Repair Shop

> Al owns an auto repair shop in a suburb of a large city. For several years he has been aware of a national chain of repair shops that has been driving small outfits like his out of business. Recently he has discovered that the chain will be opening an outlet less than a mile away from his repair shop.
>
> Al is a third generation auto mechanic. His store has been serving this neighborhood for 40 years. It has been profitable every year, and profitability has increased in the last few years. What should Al do?

**You:**    Could you begin by giving me a brief background on the automotive repair industry? Is this a fragmented industry?

*This is an industry that you're not familiar with, so feel free to ask a few explanatory questions. This is also a good time for you to begin to think about how you want to tackle this case.*

*Interviewer:*    The auto repair industry has been composed mostly of smaller units, such as Al's until recently.

*At this point, you're wondering how the national chains have managed to outcompete the smaller units. Is Al fighting a losing battle? Or is there room for both the national chains and the smaller workshops to coexist? These are the questions you want to explore. If you do find that the two businesses can coexist, then you have to determine how Al needs to change his strategy to do this.*

**You:**    What is the source of this national chain's competitive advantage?

*Interviewer:*    National chains have benefited from economies of scale. They have been especially successful at consolidating purchasing and workforce training nationally. This particular competitor has invested heavily in marketing, and has established a nationally recognized brand name.

**You:**    I would like to begin by presenting a framework in which to analyze this situation. As I see it, Al has two things to do. First, he must determine how he can successfully compete against this national chain. Second, if he concludes that he cannot compete, he must devise an exit strategy for his business.

*It is good to add the second point, because if you find that Al is not able to compete, then there are still other actions you can recommend, such as selling the business or closing down.*

*Interviewer:* Let's start with the more optimistic option.

*Customers are a good place to begin. You want to determine which customers Al might lose to the national chain, and which ones he would retain. Can he continue to run the business on the customers he retains?*

*You:* Can you tell me about Al's customers?

*Interviewer:* About half of Al's customers are individuals; the other half is comprised of private firms. Of the individual customers, 90 percent of them live within a five-mile radius of his shop. Al has a high repeat rate, as a result of his friendly and personal service.

*The next thing you want to know is how profitable the two segments are. The danger is that Al might lose the profitable customers to the national chain. Can he prevent this?*

*You:* Are both customer segments equally profitable?

*Interviewer:* The individual segment is 50 percent more profitable than the corporate one. Gross margins are 30 percent for individuals, and 20 percent for corporate customers.

*You:* How does this compare to the industry's margins?

*Interviewer:* Al enjoys much higher margins than the industry average.

*Not really a surprise, given that this neighborhood doesn't have a national chain yet – and once it does, prices and margins will probably both fall. But perhaps there are other reasons, so go ahead and ask why Al's margins are higher?*

*You:* Are the higher margins the result of higher prices charged to individuals? And if so, why is Al able to charge higher prices?

*Interviewer:* Al charges higher prices and provides a higher level of service. He provides a free vehicle and customer pickup/drop-off service, for instance. He also has free soda and snacks in his waiting room.

*You've now learned that Al does provide a higher benefit in exchange for the higher prices his customers pay. Now is a good time to ask about corporate customers.*

*You:*          What type of firms does Al serve in the corporate segment?

*Interviewer:*   A variety of different firms, such as various private businesses that contract the maintenance of their auto fleet to Al.

*You:*          What about the existing competition? Are their other repair stores in this area?

*Interviewer:*   Five years ago, there were four shops in a five mile radius. That was when Al took over from his father. Now there is only one, which is also on the brink of closure.

*This is probably part of the reason why Al can charge higher prices, and why his margins have been increasing in the last few years.*

*Another thing to consider is Al's resources. Since his shop is small, it's possible that if the national chain enters, it might steal his mechanics, in addition to his customers. It's time to determine if this might happen.*

*You:*          How many mechanics does Al have, and is there a fear of them leaving for the national chain?

*Interviewer:*   Al has 20 mechanics. On average, they have been with the shop for 15 years. They are highly proficient and loyal to Al.

*At this point, you have quite a bit of information. But you then also must come up with an additional idea about insurance companies. Since it's the insurance firms that actually pay for repairs, repair shops really have to serve two sets of clients: the customer and the insurance company. You want some information on Al's relationship with the latter.*

*You:*          Could you tell me about Al's relationship with the insurance companies?

*Interviewer:*   Al has excellent relationships with the insurance companies. Claims adjusters rely on his estimates.

*As soon as you're ready, go ahead and make an initial hypothesis. This is not your recommendation; it's an interim assessment. You can always change your hypothesis if you discover new information. Consultants often make hypotheses, so this is a familiar tactic to them.*

*You:*          I think I'm ready to present an initial assessment of the situation. Al operates in a market with relatively little competition and high margins, making it attractive to the national chain. However, Al has a loyal employee and customer base, and a strong relationship with the insurance companies.

*Interviewer:*  So do you think Al can compete against the national chain?

*Your final analysis is based on the fact that Al really cannot expect to compete on the basis of cost. So, as you speculated at the beginning of the case, he has to differentiate his business from the national chain. The one way in which you've discovered he has been doing this successfully is by providing more benefits – so go ahead and suggest that this is what he should focus on. Don't forget to mention which customers Al is more likely to retain, and that he should strengthen relationships with insurance firms.*

*You:*  I would expect the national chain has significantly lower costs than Al. I would not recommend that Al try to compete with them on price. Even if Al does try to compete on price, larger chains have both the resources and willingness to operate at low margins initially. This would surely drive Al out of business.

I suggest that Al focus on providing more value-added services to the more profitable individual segment, and shifting the focus from lower price to higher benefits to the customer. In addition, Al should reinforce his insurance relationships to increase referrals to his business. He might also establish relationships with local auto dealers and use them as a source for referrals.

It will clearly be more difficult for Al to defend his position in the corporate segment. However, Al does have the advantage over the competition, since customer retention is much cheaper than customer acquisition. While it is tempting to enter into a price war with the competition, it is ill-advised, since Al cannot possibly win. In this segment too, it is best for him to focus on adding benefits and leveraging relationships.

*Interviewer:*  Would you advise Al to exit the business?

*You:*  I do not see the need to exit a profitable business at this stage. Al has many valuable assets, such as an established reputation and valuable relationships, which he can leverage to defend himself against this competitive threat.

All the same, it might be worthwhile for Al to consider his exit options, such as selling the business, perhaps even to the national chain or a rival chain. It might even be advisable for Al to weigh the market value of his business against the discounted value of future cash flow streams. It's possible that the former might be attractive enough for him to pursue.

---

## Vault Bonus Case Analysis

This is a competitive threat case. A good place to begin would be to determine the basis of both the entrant's and the incumbent's competitive advantage. It's technically possible to find a completely lopsided situation, where one firm has a clearly superior value proposition. In the case interview context, however, you will probably find that both the entrant and the incumbent have their own strengths. If this is the case, you might want to turn your attention to segmenting the market, and identifying which segment each firm should target. In this case, the new entrant would pursue the segment which values price most; and the incumbent would continue to focus on the less price sensitive segment and provide greater value-added services.

While it is important to analyze the situation in terms of how the incumbent must react to the threat, one should not ignore the exit option. In this case, it was unnecessary, given the strengths of the incumbent. In other situations, if there is evidence that the competitive threat is severe, it would be advisable to outline various exit strategies. For example, the new competitor might be prepared to reduce its prices to a level so low that Al would lose enough of his customers to be driven out of business.

---

# Case 7: Call Me, I'm In Insurance

> Your client is an insurance provider. The company has recently acquired a number of regional companies and is now faced with the difficult task of consolidating operations. One area in which the company expected to have positive synergies from the acquisitions is in its call center operations. However, it is concerned that any disruption of its call centers might result in inconveniencing customers, even if it's only temporary. This task of consolidating the call centers is made more difficult by the number of different legacy systems in place at each call center. How would you advise the company to proceed with this integration? Or would you advise against it?

*You think you know what a call center is, but never assume anything. You had better get the interviewer to clarify.*

**You:** I would like to understand what role the call center plays in the company's business.

*Interviewer:* A call center is a customer service center. It is staffed by a number of customer service representatives, or CSRs, who field telephone calls from the company's customers.

*Next you want to try to get an idea of the scale that we're talking about here: two centers, 20 centers, or 200?*

**You:** And where are our client's customers located?

*Interviewer:* The majority of the firm's customers are in the United States.

**You:** How many different call centers does this company now have?

*Interviewer:* The company has over 20 different call centers, in various parts of the country. It employs about 500 CSRs.

*You now know the number of centers and employees, but you have also determined that the call centers are all within the United States. This is important. The case would be quite different if there were an international element to it. But you also want to clarify that having these centers located all across the United States is not important, as long as the customer is well-served.*

**You:**     And how important is geography for locating a call center? I would imagine it is not necessary for them to be located close to the customer?

*Just make sure.*

*Interviewer:*  I think that is realistic.

**You:**     Are these 24-hour locations?

*Interviewer:*  Yes, they all are.

*Now it's time to set the framework from which you're going to work on the case. There are two main questions: How many call centers does the business need, given their customer service needs? And how can it provide this customer service at the lowest cost?*

**You:**     I would like to frame this analysis as follows. First, I'd like to address the question of what is the optimal number of call centers that are necessary for the company's current business. Second, I will address the logistics of integrating the 20 centers the company currently operates.

*Interviewer:*  So, what might be an optimal number of call centers?

*Looks like you'll have to answer the first question yourself. It's not so tough. What's vital is not the number of call centers, but the number of CSRs that are needed to answer all the customer inquiries efficiently. In economic terms, you have to equate the "marginal cost per call" to the "marginal benefit of the call."*

**You:**     I think there are two important dimensions on which a call center should be judged. The cost per call, and some measure of customer satisfaction.

If the company were starting from scratch, it might be best to have just one call center. However, since it's not starting from scratch, there might be reasons to have more than one.

Minimizing the number of call centers would be beneficial for many reasons. The key cost drivers for the call centers are personnel costs, telephone expenses, and the cost of the technology infrastructure. Locating all the CSRs in one location would reduce overhead expenses, make CSR training and supervision easier, and reduce the cost of maintaining and controlling the technology support systems. Since all the centers are open 24 hours, locations becomes even less important.

Collapsing the 20 centers into a single center has the added benefit of a lower overall personnel cost. Since call volume will vary at different times and days, each individual center will have some excess CSR capacity. The excess CSR capacity required at one centralized facility will be less than cumulative excess capacity at 20 centers, for a given level of customer service.

*Interviewer:* Are you recommending that the company close 19 of its 20 centers? I would like you to discuss morale issues now.

**This is interesting; the interviewer is now turning your attention towards personnel issues. Roll with it, but be prepared to present an analysis that is based on financial considerations.**

*You:* Not without understanding some of the other factors that will also influence this decision. The decision to close call centers may be met by resistance from the employees, resulting in employee dissatisfaction and negative publicity. What is the possibility of this happening, and how can the company minimize this? Are call center employees full-time staff or temps?

*Interviewer:* Fifteen of the 20 centers only employ temps. There is some fear among staff members of the other five that they may lose their jobs.

*You:* How large are each of the five centers that employ full-time staff?

*Interviewer:* Three of them are quite small, staffed by less than 30 CSRs total. The other two are very large; each has over 50 CSRs.

*You:* Are these two large centers located close to each other?

*Interviewer:* Yes, they're located within 10 miles of each other.

*You:* What is the cost per call at these two centers?

*Interviewer:* These two centers have among the lowest cost per call of the 20. This is partly due to their size, and partly due to lower rent and salaries in this geographic area.

*You:* Do the full-time employees have any unusual skills or experience that would make them difficult to replace? Is a training program in place to ensure customer satisfaction?

*Interviewer:*  There are training programs in place at all facilities. Some of the CSRs must answer somewhat complicated questions about insurance matters, but most inquiries are routine.

*Now you have enough information to submit an initial hypothesis. Synthesize the information you've received and make a recommendation. As it turns out, the morale problem is something that might be able to be dealt with, given that most of the centers employ temps. Because the company is apparently concerned about both morale and customer satisfaction, it makes sense to try to retain some full time staff.*

*You:*  I think I'm ready to set forth an initial hypothesis. The per-call cost can be minimized by collapsing all 20 of the centers into a single center, which will be physically located at one of these two large centers. Ceasing to employ temps is unlikely to cause employee dissatisfaction. As for handling the full-time employees at the four locations with full-time employees that are to be shut down, employees could be given the option to transfer to the centralized location.

*Interviewer:*  And how will the company deal with maintaining customer satisfaction?

*This is a question that you haven't considered yet. Just how will all these centers be collapsed without disrupting regular operations? It's time to look at all the possible problems that can arise, and how they can be avoided.*

*You:*  Customer satisfaction will depend on how smoothly the company is able to consolidate all the operations. There appear to be two important factors in the call center operations: human resources, and infrastructure (both physical and technology).

We have looked at the human resource angle of the integration already. The company should allow current full-time CSRs to transfer to the central facility. The new central location should have adequate staffing levels. If new CSRs need to be hired, they should go through the training programs in place. It might be best to close one center at a time, and reroute calls to the new facility, in order to minimize the possibility of disruption.

Physical infrastructure should be expanded at the central facility. Finally, the issue of technology infrastructure should be addressed. This might be the subject of a whole new consulting study. The company might either select the most appropriate system from its current range, or choose to install an entirely new system altogether. Assuming all systems show equal customer satisfaction, however, I would select one of the systems already in place at the location to be retained to minimize retraining.

*Interviewer:* Are there any other issues you would like to mention?

*Here's where you can bring in that international aspect finally. Call centers use a lot of labor, and since wages are lower in many other English-speaking countries, it might be worthwhile for the firm to consider relocating its call center to another country, though this might impact the previously mentioned morale issue.*

*You:* Yes, I believe many companies are shifting call center operations outside of the U.S., to English-speaking countries with cheaper labor. This is an option worth investigating. However, while this might reduce the cost per call, it is important to keep in mind its impact on customer service. Many call centers in India, for example, have proven themselves proficient in providing fluent English-language customer service. But since we've already determined that training is an issue, it might be more expensive to make sure that these new centers could provide good customer service.

There's another issue that I haven't brought up at all. The call centers are currently open 24 hours a day. We should investigate whether or not it is really necessary to provide such service. Even reducing hours to 16 instead of 24 would reduce costs further.

## Vault Bonus Case Analysis

This is a typical operations consolidation case. A good place to begin is to understand the impact of the particular operations on a company's overall business. This will also help establish the key dimensions on which these operations should be evaluated. In this case, there are two metrics, one financial (cost per call), and one non-financial (customer service). It is then imperative to judge if the consolidation might improve the firm's ability to perform better on one or more dimension, while holding the other constant. In this specific case, the cost per call would be reduced, for the same level of customer satisfaction.

# Case 8: Wireless Banking

The timeframe for this case is the mid-1990s. A small division of a New York-based commercial bank has recently developed a wireless banking software. The division managers are excited about the potential of this new technology, and its impact on their business. They already have a workable beta version of the technology and are about to approach the management for a budget to develop a full-fledged version that can be deployed throughout the firm. Help them devise a business plan to leverage this new technology.

*Wireless banking software seems very complex. Go ahead and clarify what it really means? What use is this new software? Why are these managers excited about it?*

**You:** Could you tell me a little more about the software? What applications can it be used for?

**Interviewer:** This is an application that can allow banking customers to conduct transactions and access their account information wirelessly, using cell phones.

*Now you know what it does, but how large is the opportunity?*

**You:** How widely used are cell phones?

**Interviewer:** They are increasingly popular, especially among our clients, who tend to be urban and wealthy.

**You:** And is this software specific to the banking industry, or can other service providers use it as well?

**Interviewer:** This particular application has been designed to best meet the requirements of the banking industry. It is possible that other industries could copy some of the features.

*It looks like it's only the banking industry that we're talking about. Let's talk about the opportunity in the industry. Does it work? How novel is this software? What market share can it get? Who are the other competitors?*

**You:** How good is this software? Does it work?

*Interviewer:* Extensive testing has found this product convenient and easy to use.

*You:* At what stage is the penetration of wireless banking? Are other banks already offering wireless services?

*Interviewer:* Not at this time. Our client could potentially be the first to offer this service.

*If nobody else is offering these services, you have to consider two options. First, what is the value of installing the software just in the client's bank? Second, what is the value of selling the software to other banks? Which of these two options might be more profitable? Let's explore both options.*

*You:* But a first-mover advantage might be limited, since other banks would quickly offer a similar service. Can our client build any barriers to entry?

*You ask this question because if you can prevent other banks from providing the service, then this would make it a unique service, and more attractive to your client.*

*Interviewer:* Like all software products, the company could prevent other firms from outright intellectual property violation, but one cannot rule out the infiltration of clones that serve the same purpose.

*The interviewer seems to be signaling that keeping the software within the client's bank might not really release its full potential. So now let's pursue the second option of selling this software to other banks as well.*

*You:* I think I'm ready to offer a first stab at the company's strategy for this new application. The division seems to favor the idea of developing the product immediately and offering it to the bank's customers. I don't think this is the best use of the technology, because they do not have the ability to protect this innovation from being quickly copied. Any edge the bank has when it first offers this service would vanish when other banks begin to do so as well.

*Interviewer:* Are there other parallel technological innovations you can think of which have met with similar challenges?

*This is a difficult question – the interviewer is putting you on the spot. You have to think about an innovation that could be copied easily.*

*You:*  I think ATM machines are another innovation with similar characteristics.

*Interviewer:*  So what should our client do?  Does this technology have any value to it at all?

*Here's where you put forward your recommendation: You've determined that the bank will not be able to keep other banks from quickly developing similar services, so it is best for them instead to go ahead and sell the software to competing banks. Banks will buy this software because it has apparent value, and it's worth buying rather than wasting time and resources redeveloping it.  This has the additional advantage of making your client's software the template for other such systems. And your client would still have a head start.*

*You:*  The technology certainly has value.  I would recommend that the client deploy it within the firm, but simultaneously license the technology solution to other banks.  This is where the real value lies.

The value proposition to other banks is that they would not have to invest the dollars and time in developing or procuring this solution themselves.  Our client must accept that if it does not offer its solution to the competition, somebody else will, and that will place our client at a disadvantage.  It is therefore best for our client to capture as much of this market as possible, perhaps by spinning off the technology using a subsidiary independent from its banking parent.

*Interviewer:*  But our client then would not get the benefit of being the only bank to offer this service.

*You've already thought through this argument, so go ahead and make it explicit. It's really a choice between two positive value options – the licensing option has the higher value, compared to the internal deployment.*

*You:*  This is correct.  Selling the software would limit first-mover advantage.  However, it is clear from the facts that this is not a defensible technological advantage.  Other banks will soon copy this innovation, regardless of whether our client chooses to sell them its solution or not.

The additional profit from a few additional months of being the only bank to offer this service has to be compared with the profits to be made from selling this solution to other banks.  Since wireless banking is a new way of banking, our client would have to educate customers on how to use this service. Profits in the first few months or even years would be limited. This is why the licensing option is preferable. Overall, the bank should consider the ROI (return on investment) measure, rather than absolute profits in dollars, since ROI captures both the initial investment, as well as the income that the investment generates.

Finally, since this is a virgin market, having other banks offering wireless services would grow the market for wireless banking services faster than if our client went at it on its own. Licensing the software also lessens the danger that an alternate standard platform for wireless banking will arise, which could potentially force our client to scrap the current model.

## Vault Bonus Case Analysis

This case is based on a popular business school theme: how to deal with innovation. In this case, the licensing option is preferable because of the low defensibility of the technology. It is important to note how towards the end of the case the interviewer pushes you. Unless compelling new information is introduced, stick to your recommendation.

# Case 9: Car Manufacturer

> An Asian car manufacturer currently offers two models in the U.S. market: one mid-level car, and one high-end. It is considering introducing an entry-level car in the U.S. that it is already selling in various foreign markets. However, these are in markets with different competitors and brands.
>
> In the U.S., there are numerous entry-level cars available for sale. The company would like you to create a positioning strategy for its entry-level model.

*It is not clear what the interviewer means by entry-level cars. You have a feeling it has to do with price, but it might include other factors. It's better to clarify.*

**You:** I would like to start by clarifying the definition of an "entry-level" car. Is this a categorization based solely on price?

*Interviewer:* No, price is not the only factor. "Entry-level" can be defined on a number of dimensions: type of buyer, standard versus extra options, technical specifications, and price, among other factors. However, for the sake of convenience, let's assume price is the most significant.

*Now you would like to set up the framework for the discussion. The important issues to consider in a market entry case – which is what this is – are all the factors that will influence the pricing decisions. The key external factors are customers and competition.*

**You:** I'd like to look at the following issues in this analysis: the competition, customers, and finally the various facets of a positioning strategy.

*Interviewer:* Fine.

*You can start by asking about the different cars and companies that our client will compete with first.*

**You:** Could you please tell me a little about the competition the company expects to face at the entry-level level?

*Interviewer:* You can rely on your knowledge of the United States car market.

*Better draw on your own knowledge of the car market. The interviewer should let you know, either verbally or non-verbally, that you're on the right track.*

*You:* I'm thinking of Neons, Hyundai Accents, Saturns – that level of car, with a price ranging between $10,000 and $15,000.

*Interviewer:* That sounds OK.

*Now that you know that you're in this kind of market, you're more comfortable with this case. Now you need more information on your customers. How do they select a car?*

*You:* How do our client's cars differ from the competition? On what factors do the existing mid- and high-level models compete?

*Interviewer:* The company prides itself on providing maximum value to the customer.

*Now don't jump to conclusions! You know the strategic concept of value – the difference between benefit and price – but you want to make sure the company doesn't define it differently.*

*You:* And how does it define value?

*Interviewer:* How would you define value?

*If the company had its own definition for value, the interviewer would have probably revealed it. Then again, the interviewer might just be curious to hear what you have to say. Go ahead and apply your definition of value to entry-level cars.*

*You:* Value would be the difference between the perceived benefit of the car and the price that is paid for it. While price is easy to measure, benefit is more troublesome. For a car, value would be a function of a number of attributes: quality, design, brand, specifications, comfort, capacity, maintenance plan and so on. A market research survey can be carried out to measure the value customers would place on a mix of these various attributes. Has the company attempted to carry out any market research to measure perceived benefits?

*Interviewer:* Yes, the company has estimates of benefits as a the result of some focus groups it ran recently. Here is a table that gives price (as paid by the consumer) and benefit data for the top three competitors.

| | Competitor 1 | Competitor 2 | Competitor 3 | Our Client |
|---|---|---|---|---|
| Price | 10,000 | 12,000 | 15,000 | ? |
| Benefit | 12,000 | 15,000 | 16,500 | 11,000 |

*This is excellent! You now know the "value" that each of the competitor's models provides. You can work backwards to compute the price for our client's model based on the second competitor's value calculation – since it currently provides the highest value to customers.*

**You:**      From this data, competitor 2 provides the highest value, $3,000. Our client would have to price its model below $8,000 in order to provide a higher value to its customers. Given its cost base, is this realistic?

*Interviewer:*   Why is it necessary to consider cost in making a positioning decision?

*This is an easy question. Of course, cost matters, because it's possible that the firm's cost is higher than $8,000, in which case it cannot price it at that level. But you're already thinking ahead. What if this is the case? Then the company could try to lower costs. Or it could try to increase the perceived benefits.*

**You:**      Cost would impact the company's profitability. The optimal pricing decision would actually depend on an estimate of the demand elasticity for this car model. I would recommend that the company increase its market research efforts to estimate demand at different price points.

While the value analysis is useful to provide a benchmark price, the precise price would maximize profitability, given the estimated quantity demanded.

The cost is also important to consider because the company may not be in a position to extend its value maximization strategy to this model, if for instance, this model costs $9,000 to produce.

*Interviewer:*   What should the company do if value maximization is not possible because of a higher cost structure?

*Good. You were expecting this question, and you've already thought it through. Go ahead and present the two options you were considering earlier.*

*You:*    There are at least two things the company might be able to do. The obvious thing is to try to reduce costs. An analysis of the various cost components, such as production costs, shipping and transportation, distribution, marketing and advertising would be a good place to begin.

A second option would be to try to raise the perceived benefit to the customer. This might be possible through improved marketing. It is also possible to add product features to the vehicle that cost less than the incremental perceived benefit. Once again this is a marketing research problem: What is the optimal combination of product features which results in the highest increase in benefit, for the lowest increase in product cost? Third, the company might simply attempt to compete on price and not value, as the cost of its entry-level model is the lowest of all cars at its level.

*Interviewer:*    Are there other issues that the company should consider?

*Here's where you can demonstrate your creativity. Take a few seconds to gather your thoughts if you'd like. There are many additional issues that can be discussed here. You can discuss the fact that the firm could use its experience in selling the entry-level model in other markets. You can also talk about the fact that introducing an additional model has cost benefits: lower overall distribution costs, since the firm already has established distributors; lower advertising and promotion costs perhaps, especially related to overall brand building. With the addition of an entry-level car, the firm can also provide its customers with an option at every stage of life, and try to retain them for their entire lifetimes – beginning with selling them an entry level model, and then presenting them with higher options as they become ready to trade up. You can discuss any of these issues.*

*You:*    Yes, a couple of other issues come to mind. The company could cater to customers buying their first car, and then work on graduating them up to higher end models later in life. A negative impact might be some risk of cannibalization with other models, but considering the entry-level model would probably cater to a different customer segment, I would expect the impact of this to be quite low indeed.

A second issue is the fact that the company already sells the entry-level car in foreign markets. It might draw on its experience in those markets, look at the value calculations there, anticipate competitive actions and so on.

## Vault Bonus Case Analysis

This case focuses on a core strategic concept: value. "Value" is a very important concept – it is the difference between benefit and price. Value, or net benefit, is a good predictor of market share. It is very likely that a product that provides the highest value to its customers will also have the highest market share – all else being equal, of course!

Value as applied to the context of the case is the difference between the benefit to the customer and the price the customer pays for a specific car. The latter is easily determined. The former, benefit, can be determined by a marketing study that ascertains how much a customer would be willing to pay for the mix of the various attributes of a particular model (design, specifications, interior, brand, etc.).

In addition, a company can attempt to shift the perceived benefit to the customer by effective advertising, and by changing the product bundle to include features more important to the target audience. For example, a younger car-buying audience might value a stereo system over side impact airbags or built-in child safety seats, even though the stereo might technically be the least "valuable" of the three.

# Case 10: Bill, Bill, Bill

> Your client is an established law firm in a large U.S. city. The firm currently charges its clients an hourly fee. It is, however, considering changing to a fixed fee. The firm is considering the change because a flat fee reduces administrative costs and is preferred by some clients. The firm is apprehensive that a fixed fee might result in lower profitability for the firm.
>
> What are the pros and cons of making this change in billing policy? Is the firm correct in believing profitability will be hurt by this change?

*The first thing you want to do is probe into whether this is really a change driven by the firm's clients? Or has a one-off comment prompted this study?*

**You:** Do all the firm's clients support the move to a fixed fee?

**Interviewer:** No, only a portion of them. Say, half of them would want a fixed fee.

*Fifty percent is a significant percentage, so this isn't something you can dismiss lightly. You know that monitoring the number of hours is used for external billing, but also for internal considerations, such as internal expenses and law firm associate evaluations. For example, law firms often base bonuses for lawyers on the number of hours billed.*

**You:** Would changing the system from an hourly fee to a fixed fee have an impact on internal tracking of how many lawyer-hours were spent on a case?

**Interviewer:** No, our client has decided that it will continue to track lawyers' hours regardless of any changes to billing.

*Now you can lay out your plan of attack. First, you want to talk about the firm's clients and its billing system. Second, you want to talk about internal expenses and evaluations. Finally and most importantly, you must talk about the impact on profitability – after all, you want to ensure that a change in the billing system will not harm profitability.*

**You:** I would like to structure this discussion by focusing on the aspects this change will have on three areas: clients, the internal performance appraisal system, and profitability.

*Interviewer:*   Fine.

*You realize that you have to consider the variation in the hours that are spent on a case. It's very difficult to accurately predict how many hours a case will take. With an hourly system, the law firm really doesn't care about making accurate predictions – it gets paid for the actual hours it works. But with a fixed system, it's necessary to make accurate predictions.*

*You:*   The impact on clients would be as follows. Each case will have some sort of distribution around the mean number of hours. Sometimes the actual number of hours will be greater than the mean, and sometimes less. On average, a client who uses the law firm's service regularly will be billed on the mean number of hours (M).

With an hourly fee, it is the client who bears the risk of variation in the number of hours required for a case. With a fixed fee, the law firm would assume this risk by guaranteeing its client a fixed cost.

Should the law firm decide to charge a fixed fee, I would recommend that it base the fixed fee on M + some extra wiggle room, or (E). The E might be considered compensation for the extra risk that the law firm would bear, because under a fixed fee the variability risk transfers from the client to the law firm.

*Interviewer:*   What impact would this have on profitability?

*You:*   If the law firm charges M+E, where E is the extra compensation for the added variability risk, the firm's profits will increase because the average number of hours incurred would still be M.

However, this cannot really be considered "additional profit" because it is essentially compensation for the higher level of business risk that the law firm is volunteering to take.

*Interviewer:*   How will the firm arrive at the appropriate E?

*Determining E is difficult, but it can be done using a combination of statistical analysis and good judgment.*

*You:*   That's a good question, because it's definitely not a precise science. I think there are a number of ways in which the firm can compute E. It could do a statistical analysis of its past cases, especially if it maintains records of the initial expectation of M before the case began, and the final number of hours actually incurred at the end of the case. A statistical analysis would reveal the margin of error. If it doesn't have much historical data, the best thing to do would be to use its experience and judgment initially, but fine tune it as it collects more data. One thing is clear: it will be necessary for our client to invest in conducting statistical analysis on an ongoing basis.

*Interviewer:* You mentioned an impact on performance appraisal? Why?

*So now you can move on to the impact on the lawyers and on performance appraisal. You want to make sure that lawyers' hours continue to be recorded for this purpose, even if the firm decides to switch to a fixed fee system.*

*You:* From the little I know about professional service organizations, such as law firms, the number of hours invested in a project by a lawyer is a key internal metric. I believe many law firms have a minimum number of billable hours that a lawyer must generate annually. This system essentially utilizes billable hours as a proxy for performance. In the absence of an hourly billing system, there might be a lower motivation with the firm to maintain accurate billable hour statistics, therefore impairing the firm's ability to appraise the performance of individual lawyers. Of course, if the firm continues to track billable hours, this is less of a consideration.

*Interviewer:* What would you recommend our client should do?

*You've established that there is significant customer demand for a fixed fee system. You also recommended how the firm can develop one. You just need to summarize what you've said so far and make a solid recommendation.*

*You:* I would recommend that the firm segment its client base into those that are willing to take the risk of an hourly rate, and those that are not. They might consider offering a fixed fee to the latter segment, but at a premium, as described earlier.

*Interviewer:* Are there any other problems you expect with a fixed fee system?

*The one problem with the fixed fee system is contained in the economics concept of "adverse selection." Adverse selection occurs when one party to a transaction has information that the other doesn't. The owner of this information does not have an incentive to share it with the other party, if sharing it will adversely impact the informed party.*

*You:*      Yes, there is always the problem of adverse selection or hidden information.   Generally the law firm will have a better understanding of the number of hours necessary to work on a specific type of case.  However, before the casework begins, the client might have an incentive to conceal information that might increase the number of hours required in actuality.  Our client will have to incorporate the appropriate clauses into the contract that allow it to increase its fees, should additional information about the case become available after the initial appraisal and fixed fee offer.

The insurance industry faces a similar problem; individuals with medical problems are more motivated to purchase medical or life insurance than those who are healthy.

---

## Vault Bonus Case Analysis

This case exposes two important concepts.  The first is the relationship between risk and return.  In efficient markets, higher risk is associated with a risk premium, and a corresponding return.  The difference between the hourly fee and a fixed fee can be interpreted in this context.

A second concept invoked in this case is that of adverse selection.  The differential information ownership causes a perverse effect, as the party with the greater information is capable of using this to its advantage.  For example, people with chronic illnesses are more likely to sign up for health insurance plans that permit unlimited office visits.

---

# Case 11: Wilting Profits

A landscape construction company has recently hired us to study the causes for its declining profitability. The company is 30 years old, and has increased revenues and profits annually for most of this period. In the last three years, however, profits have begun to decline.

Your task is to try to determine the cause, or causes, for this decline.

*You're not exactly sure what "landscape construction" means, so ask!*

**You:** I would like to try to understand what a landscape construction company actually does. Does it do the initial irrigation and earth works? Does it do landscape maintenance work?

*Interviewer:* Yes to both.

*You've been told that profits are declining. Profits can decline for two reasons: either revenues are declining or costs are increasing. So, let's test both possibilities.*

**You:** Have revenues been declining as well?

*Interviewer:* No. Revenues have increased by 5 percent every year for the last three years.

*If it's not a revenue issue, it must be a cost issue. Try to find out what exactly is costing too much. After identifying the costs, you might be able to suggest a way to reverse this trend.*

*Costs consist of fixed costs and variable costs. The former are "fixed" regardless of the level of revenues; and the latter vary with revenues.*

**You:** What about the company's cost structure? Has there been an increase in fixed costs?

*Interviewer:* Fixed costs have increased, but at a lower rate than the growth in revenues. Fixed costs as a percentage of revenues have actually declined.

*Good, so it's the variable costs that are the problem. Test this hypothesis. Three main variable costs are labor, materials and equipment.*

**You:** Then perhaps there has been an increase in variable costs. I would imagine that labor, materials and equipment are the major variable cost components.  Has there been a significant change in wage rates?  Are material prices higher?  Or is the company using more expensive equipment?

*Interviewer:*   I'm afraid none of these things have happened.  In fact, the company recently renegotiated wages with the union.  Hourly wage rates have declined from $15.35 to $15.00 as a result of the recent economic slowdown.  In addition, material prices have also dropped marginally.  And there have been no substantial changes in the equipment the company uses.

*This seems like a tough case.  Revenues are rising, but costs are not.  However, while total revenues are rising, it's still possible that the revenues per unit are not.  In other word, it's possible that margins are declining for some reason.  You can probe the competitive environment to see if you can identify any reason why this might occur.*

*You:*   Well, we've been through all of the prospective internal effects that might negatively impact profitability.  I would like to turn my attention to the external environment the company is operating in.  I would like to test the hypothesis that increased competition is affecting the prices our client is able to charge in the market.

Have there been any new entrants into our client's market?  Or are existing competitors reducing prices?

*Interviewer:*   I'm afraid neither of these is the case.  There have been no new entrants into our client's core market, and the established competitors are not reducing prices.

*Looks like there's no new competitive pressure on prices.  Any decline in revenues per unit must be a decision made by the company.  For instance, it's possible that prices have been reduced intentionally to increase volumes.  Or the decline in margins is the result of a change in product mix.  Test both hypotheses.*

*You:*   You referred to our client's "core" market.  What are the different markets, or customer segments, that the company does business in?

*Interviewer:*   The company has identified three major customer segments.  The so-called core segment is "recreational landscaping," large new landscape construction projects, such as gardens, parks and golf courses.  A second segment, "residential landscaping," refers to new landscaping projects for private residences.  A third segment, "landscaping maintenance," is the ongoing maintenance required for existing properties. This is a new segment the company ventured into about four years ago.

*Perhaps the product mix hypothesis is appropriate here. You need to pursue this idea further. If the company has been expanding its presence in a lower margin segment, it could account for the decline in profitability.*

*You:* What percentage of revenues do each of the three segments constitute?

*Interviewer:* Here is some information on revenue shares:

|  | Year 1 | Year 2 | Year 3 |
|---|---|---|---|
| Recreational | 80% | 80% | 70% |
| Residential | 14% | 15% | 15% |
| Maintenance | 6% | 5% | 15% |

*This is enough for a hypothesis.*

*You:* My current hypothesis is that the maintenance segment has lower margins than the other two. The recent growth rate in this segment is reducing the overall profitability of the firm.

*Interviewer:* That would be correct. So should the company continue to grow the maintenance segment?

*You were right. So the question now is: Are current low margins worth it for a longer term gain in market share? An ROI-like metric would be an appropriate measure here.*

*You:* The answer to this question depends. Profitability is defined by net income as a percentage of revenues. Using this metric alone has certain pitfalls. It does not indicate return on investment, for instance. It is possible that while profitability is lower, the maintenance has a higher ROI, or higher return on assets. I also haven't asked you whether profits are rising in the maintenance sector, which could indicate a positive trend.

*Interviewer:* Are there any other reasons, other than financial reasons, to continue to serve the maintenance market?

*Yes, there are a number of reasons. Be creative.*

*You:*          Yes, I can think of other reasons. First, it is possible that margins might improve with economies of scale, as the maintenance division grows. Maintenance services allow the company to nurture a constant relationship with its clients, and might enable it to win future construction contracts as well. Maintenance might also be a more stable business, which would allow the firm to weather economic downturns more easily.

---

## Vault Bonus Case Analysis

This is a classic declining profitability case. The first part of this case dealt with solving this puzzle. It is important to keep in mind the basic determinants of profit in a firm (profit = revenues less costs) when working through this puzzle. Explore all the reasons why costs might have increased, and revenues declined, until you find the solution.

The second part of this case questions the use of profitability as a performance measure. It is important to remember that there are instances when poor profitability is offset by other benefits, as described in this case.

---

# Case 12: A Time For Marketing Strategy

Your client markets brand name watches in the $100 to $1,000 price range. Prior to the ubiquity of the Internet, the company distributed its watches through two channels: department stores and specialty watch stores. In the last few years, it has also been offering an online store on its website, which allows it to sell directly to customers. In addition, it has authorized a limited number of online stores to also carry its watches.

Online purchases have increased dramatically in the last year to the extent that the firm's traditional channels, the department stores and the specialty stores, have begun to object vehemently. What can the firm to do resolve this channel conflict?

*This is a typical channel conflict situation, where the manufacturer is burdened with managing conflict among its channel partners or distributors. The first issue to ascertain here is how important are the different channels to our client. One way to do this is to look at data on "channel share" trends, or the proportion of watches that flow through the different channels.*

*You:* Do we have any data available on the share of watches that are sold through the different channels?

*Interviewer:* Yes, we have data for the last three years.

| | Year 1 | Year 2 | Year 3 |
|---|---|---|---|
| Department Stores | 80% | 79% | 78% |
| Specialty Stores | 19% | 18% | 15% |
| Online Retailers | < 1% | 3% | 7% |

*This is useful data. It is clear that the online channel, while still miniscule, is growing rapidly. The next thing to determine is the extent of the competition. While it's possible that the different channels meet the needs of differing customer segments, there is often overlap. Plus, you need to determine on what dimensions the distributors compete: cost, retail price, service and so on. You can start with cost and price.*

**You:** And does our client follow a differential pricing strategy for each of the three channels?

*Interviewer:* The firm offers volume discounts, irrespective of the buyer. As a result, wholesale prices to the department stores, which account for the bulk of sales, are 5 to 10 percent less than to specialty stores. Online retailers pay higher prices than both of the other two, since they move the smallest volumes.

*You now know that the different distributors have different cost structures. It's strange that the department stores and specialty stores should complain when they are buying the watches at a lower price than the online stores. Either the online stores are working on slim margins to compete, or they're selling to a different customer segment.*

**You:** I would imagine that retail prices are different across the three channels. Is that true?

*Interviewer:* Yes, they are. The specialty stores have the highest retail prices, followed by the department stores, which are about 5 percent cheaper. The online retailers price the watches at about the same price as the department stores.

*There doesn't appear to be much basis for cutthroat pricing. So, it's time to explore other reasons the online share is increasing. It might be due to a growth in the number of customers who prefer to purchase online; but before you explore that hypothesis, let's rule out the possibility that our client is not aiding this growth of online sales by investing more heavily in advertising and promotion for online stores.*

**You:** How does the firm allocate its sales and marketing budget? What proportion of its marketing and sales dollars is it allocating to each of the three channels?

*Interviewer:* Marketing budgets are mostly focused at building the brand, with only limited channel specific advertising. The company's channel partners sometimes choose to advertise the brand as well, but this is an independent decision. Sales force allocations are done more or less proportional to channel shares.

What other information do you need before you can give me your first take on a hypothesis?

*It doesn't look like sales and marketing are driving online sales either.*

**You:**   I'd like to know a little about the company's customers and its preferences. First, are there different customer segments?

**Interviewer:**   Yes, the firm has classified customers into three segments. Here are some details on each segment

| Segment | 1 | 2 | 3 |
|---|---|---|---|
| Price Range | $100 to 200 | $200 to 500 | $500 and above |

*Good, so you've got information on different segments. The next obvious question is about customer preference for different channels.*

**You:**   Do these three segments differ in their preferences for channels?

**Interviewer:**   Yes, there are two noticeable trends. First, all three segments have exhibited an interest in purchasing online — an increasing percentage of each segment have been purchasing online. Second, segment 1 has shown a particularly higher interest in online purchases when compared to the other segments.

*Touché. Looks like you've found the reason for the increase in online sales – it's due to changing customer preferences. This is an exogenous change – it's not something that either our client, or its channel partners, have control over. It's a trend they will have to adapt to. In other words, the online channel is here to stay. Our client should attempt to align the different channels with the different customer segments.*

**You:**   Ideally our client should meet customer preferences for distribution channels. In this case, the company should leverage its online channel presence to target segment 1, while refocusing the other two channels on the 2nd and 3rd segments.

**Interviewer:**   How will this resolve the grievances the department and specialty stores have expressed?

*You can't expect to align the channels without facing resistance from them. Nobody likes to lose market share.*

**You:**   I think their grievance is misdirected. Our client has little control over buying behavior. All it can do is make products available at the preferred locations for each of its three consumer segments.

However, our client might adopt a channel differentiation strategy by focusing channels towards specific segments. For instance, it might run ad campaigns with the department and specialty stores that target segments 2 and 3, while running different campaigns with the online stores to target segment 1.

*Interviewer:* So could you summarize your recommendation for me?

*In addition to the summary, there may be some concessions that our client can make to appease its channel partners; this is the time to get creative and include these in your recommendation. The client could reduce or eliminate the company-owned web site completely. It could also restrict sales on the web site to only the lower end watches. And it could help its channel partners develop online stores.*

**You:** Our client is facing a situation where the rules of the game have changed. The emergence of a new low-cost distribution channel has led to increased competition. Overall, this is a positive development for our client, since the watches are available to a wider variety of customers.

*Interviewer:* Is there an alternative to discontinuing online sales that might be acceptable to the client's other channels?

**You:** Yes, there is. Our client could restrict its online sales to segment 1, which has the highest propensity to buy online. Simultaneously, it could encourage its channel partners to establish online stores themselves. This proposal might be acceptable to their distributors for two reasons. First, segment 1 watches are the cheapest; although we would have to look at the relative volumes of the three segments. Second, this proposal involves helping the distributors build online capacities themselves. A third possibility is that the bulk of online sales are coming from locations where the other channels do not exist. If this is true, this should alleviate the concerns of the distributors.

## Vault Bonus Case Analysis

This is an example of a channel conflict case, but it also addresses the additional issue of market segmentation as well. An analysis of the pros and cons of utilizing different channels is a good starting point. Two important issues to consider are the profitability of different channels, and fit with consumer buying behavior.

# Case 13: Manufacturing out of a Paper Bag

> Your client is a paper bag manufacturing company. It manufactures a variety of paper bags in different sizes, thickness and specifications. Its products have a wide range of uses, from carrying milk in cartons to cement in 50-pound bags.
>
> The company has been experiencing a declining return on equity recently, and is unable to determine the cause for the decline. The scope of your engagement is to identify what is driving this decline, and help resolve it.

*This is an investigative case. The objective is to research what is driving the decline in ROE and present ways to resolve it. ROE can decrease either because of a decline in the numerator – "returns" – or because of an increase in the denominator – the "equity." Let's explore each reason in turn first.*

**You:** I'd like to dismiss the most obvious cause for a decline in ROE; has there been an increase in the company's equity base recently?

**Interviewer:** No. In addition, the company has been paying out most of its net income in dividends, so the total equity has remained constant for the last few years.

*So, there is a decline in "return" or net income. Net income can drop as a result of a decline in revenues, or an increase in costs.*

**You:** So, net income has been declining. Have revenues been declining as well?

**Interviewer:** Revenues have been increasing about 2 to 3 percent annually.

*If revenues have been increasing, then costs must be rising for net income to decline. One way to categorize costs is to divide them into fixed costs and variable costs. The former don't vary with revenues, while the latter do.*

**You:** Do we have any information on the fixed and variable costs? How have fixed costs changed?

**Interviewer:** Fixed costs as a percentage of revenues have remained constant.

**You:** So, variable costs have been rising?

*Interviewer:* Yes, variable costs per unit.

*You've narrowed the problem to variable costs. Two key variable costs in a manufacturing company are labor and materials, so let's explore each of these first.*

**You:** I would imagine the key components of variable cost at this firm are material and labor. Have material prices increased? Or have labor rates?

*Interviewer:* Neither has changed.

*OK, so this is getting a little complicated. If neither the materials nor the labor prices have changed, then either the quantities of materials or the cost of labor used for every unit of production have increased. This might happen due to waste or some inefficiency, or a decline in productivity. One clue might be a significant change of some sorts: in operations processes, an increase in the number of SKUs (stock keeping units) perhaps.*

**You:** I'd like to take a step back and talk about the company's products. You mentioned an expansive product range?

*Interviewer:* Yes, the company manufactures over 10,000 SKUs.

**You:** Has this always been the case? Has there been an increase in the number of SKUs recently?

*Interviewer:* Yes, in the last three years the number of SKUs has increased from 3,000 to 10,000.

*An increase in SKUs for a manufacturing company can be the cause of a decline in productivity, stemming from changeover times of equipment. Let's see if this increase in SKUs has been worth it for the company.*

**You:** Why has the company been doing this?

*Interviewer:* In order to target new market segments.

**You:** Are all of these segments profitable? Or to ask this question differently, how many of these additional SKUs are profitable?

*Interviewer:* Very few of the new products are profitable, unfortunately. The company is perplexed because the actual cost of production is much higher than it had estimated, and this is why many products remain unprofitable.

*Good, that's what you expected. This change in the number of SKUs is probably driving the increase in costs as a result of higher changeover times and lower "throughput" – the volume of production that a factory can produce in a given period of time. It's time to offer this as a hypothesis and test it.*

**You:**       I would like to propose a hypothesis, but before I do, could you tell me if the company has bought additional plants and equipment to manufacture these new products?

*Interviewer:* No, it has been using capacity at its existing plant

**You:**       I think the tripled increase in the number of SKUs is increasing changeover time, which is the time taken for a particular piece of equipment to stop the production of one product, and start the production of another. The increased changeover time is reducing the overall capacity of the plant. Since fewer products are produced, the cost per product increases.

This hypothesis is supported by the fact that neither material prices nor labor rates have changed. The variable cost per unit, however, has changed, because the total number of units has declined.

*Interviewer:* Where would you look for symptoms of this increase in changeover time you suggest?

*The symptoms would be found in the lower throughput, and therefore higher cost per unit of production. And the higher changeovers might also result in increased labor usage.*

**You:**       The increased changeover time would manifest itself in a number of increased costs. First, labor cost as a proportion of total product cost might have increased, if the changeovers are manual. Second, the throughput – or the number of product unit equivalents that the plant can produce in a given period of time – has probably declined since the increase in SKUs. Third, it is quite probable that the margins of all products, including the old, profitable ones, have fallen because the introduction of the new products has reduced total throughput.

*Interviewer:* What do you recommend the company do?

*Good. Now that we know the problem, prescribing a solution is relatively straightforward. The company must discontinue the unprofitable products that are burdening the system. Simultaneously, it needs to consider an operational audit to detect and eliminate bottlenecks and revive throughput.*

*You:*  I would recommend that the company compute the profitability of each product, considering the changeover times involved in their manufacture. They should consider discontinuing the most unprofitable products. In addition, the company can assess process flows in the factory with a view toward minimizing changeover times and increasing throughput.

*Interviewer:* What do you mean by assessing process flows?

*You:*  A process flow analysis would chart the entire manufacturing process, especially focusing on matching the capacities of different equipment to ensure that there are no bottlenecks. The throughput of a factory is as high as the throughput of its slowest machine. For instance, if changeover times are especially high for one machine, the company might consider adding more of those machines.

---

## Vault Bonus Case Analysis

This case is an operations case in the guise of a profitability case. The first part of the case probes the reasons for the poor profitability at the company. When this line of reasoning reaches a dead end, the interviewee considers the alternative of assessing the operational efficiency at the factory.

There are several clues the interviewer offers that this might be an operations case. The large range of products is an important clue. A second, less obvious, clue is when halfway through the case the candidate realizes that variable costs per unit are rising, not due to rising variable costs, but due to the number of units produced.

---

# Case 14: Low on Batteries

> A battery manufacturer in the U.K. is experiencing declining sales
> volume, even though its product is superior in lifetime and quality to
> those of its competitors. How would you approach this issue?

*A decline in sales volume can be caused by two factors: declining market
demand or loss of market share. Loss of market share can be due to competing
products or substitute products. The Porter's Five Forces framework could be
used here. Think logically about a good way to approach the problem.*

*Don't forget that you can always take some time out at the beginning to think
about your approach. Many candidates don't realize that it is perfectly fine to be
silent for a moment; this might make you look thoughtful and is much better than
starting to ramble and run around in circles. Just remember to say, "I'd like to
take a minute to gather my thoughts," before going silent!*

**You:**        What is the product, who are the customers, and who are the
competitors?

**Interviewer:**  The company sells batteries for forklifts. Sales are made to OEMs
(i.e., forklift manufacturers) and for replacement purposes to large
manufacturers and distributors who use forklifts. The majority of
sales are to the latter. Customers are located throughout Europe.
There are five or six other European manufacturers which are
similar in size to our client.

> ***Since the competitors are in different countries, the methods of manufacturing,
> labor, costs, and so on, should vary from country to country. You should keep this
> in mind, since this information will become extremely handy later in the case.***

**You:**        What is the trend in market demand?

**Interviewer:**  Demand tends to be very stable, growing at approximately 3
percent per year.

**You:**        Interesting. Since demand is stable, I can infer that the industry as
a whole is doing rather well, and that the decline in sales for the
client, therefore, is most likely due to declining market share. Let
me pursue this a little further. Are there any new substitute
products or new competitors or new technological advances in
battery manufacturing?

*Interviewer:*   There have been no major changes in technology. The only large change in the market place is the emergence of a new Portuguese competitor. This company has managed to grow to approximately the same size as our client in a relatively short period of time.

*Now you know the reason for the decline in market share. The industry analysis part is complete and you should now target the specific competitor with respect to the product and price.*

*You:*   Next, I would like to find out how this new competitor has been able to accumulate market share so quickly in an otherwise stable industry. It is necessary to evaluate the competitor's price/product proposition to compare it to our client's.

*Interviewer:*   Our client's product is superior in lifetime and quality to that of the Portuguese competitor. Our price is higher as well, however, but we feel the additional quality more than makes up for this differential.

*Looks like a price war. You must convince your client's potential customers that your client's battery is a better value, despite costing more.*

*You:*   Now that we have established the different value propositions of the two companies, we need to find out what the customer is looking for when purchasing a forklift battery. Reliability and pricing are the most likely factors for an industrial buyer, and while we outperform our competitor on the former, we are lagging on the latter. The next step would be to evaluate the trade-offs between these two attributes, and to verify our client's claim that the increased quality is worth the price.

*Interviewer:*   That sounds fine. Where would you like to start?

*You:*   First, we know that our client's product lasts longer. How much longer?

*Interviewer:*   Our battery lasts for a total of five years, while our competitor's only lasts for four years.

*You:*   And what is the price differential?

*Interviewer:*   Our battery costs £1,500, while our competitor's costs £800.

*You:*   That means that the cost per year is £1,500/5 = £300 for our product and £800/4 = £200 for the competitor's. That is not looking good on the surface. Maybe our client should reduce its prices. Does its cost base enable it to do so while maintaining an acceptable level of profitability?

*Interviewer:* Not really. Our client's cost base is substantially higher due to the higher quality of its products. In addition, labor expenses are significantly higher in the U.K. than in Portugal. Our client is not willing to leave his lukewarm Guinness and jellied eel behind, however, so moving is not an option. Therefore, lowering costs is not an option.

**You:** So far we have only considered the purchase price as a cost of the product. It is possible that there are additional costs involved. To find out, we need to evaluate the use of the batteries.

*You don't need to be an engineer to figure this out; just use your common sense. At the same time, state your assumptions.*

Forklifts will most likely ride around a plant or warehouse moving goods around. The battery powers the forklift, so it will need to be recharged periodically.

*Again, you may be completely oblivious of the fact that forklifts are used for moving goods around. Never mind. All you need to know is that the batteries need to be recharged at some point.*

While the battery is recharging, the forklift will likely be out of commission. At the very least, the battery will need to be switched, which takes time. Is there any difference in charging time or efficiency between the competing batteries?

*Interviewer:* It takes eight hours to fully charge our battery, which will then last for 12 hours. Our competitor's battery takes 10 hours to charge and can be used for 10 hours. The batteries draw the same amount of electricity per hour while charging, but due to the better design of our battery, output efficiency is higher.

**You:** This strikes me as the most crucial point, that the output efficiency of the client's product is better than that of the competitor. This efficiency difference needs to be translated into costs and value for the customer. Value is derived from lower energy requirements, faster turn-around time, and fewer switching operations. Given the fact that our client's customers are large industrial companies, they probably work around the clock. Therefore, let's assume a 24-hour-a-day need for the forklifts.

First, let's evaluate the energy savings. We need to know the price of electricity drawn per hour.

*Interviewer:* Right. Assume that the hourly rate is £.10.

**You:** If the forklift will be used 24 hours per day for, say, 350 days in a year, it will require 24/12 x 350 = 700 charges of 8 hours each for our battery. That is 5,600 hours at £.10 or £560 per year. For our competitor, the battery requires 24/10 x 350 charges of 10 hours each per year. This equals 8,400 hours or £840 per year. The difference is £280 per year per battery.

Next, let's evaluate the switching costs. I would like to know how long it takes to switch the battery.

*Interviewer:* This takes only a couple of minutes. For simplicity, let's assume the time is negligible.

**You:** That means that we can assume switching costs to be negligible. Since the batteries are out of commission while charging, however, we will need to evaluate how many batteries we need per forklift. Assume that our client's customers operate fleets with multiple forklifts, which can all share the same batteries. For our battery, each forklift requires one battery to move while another is charging for 8 of the 12 moving hours or 2/3. That means that we need 1 2/3 batteries per forklift. For our competitor's battery, the battery is charging for the entire moving time. That means that there are two batteries required for each forklift. The annual purchase cost per forklift is therefore £300 x 1 2/3 (£500) for us and £200 x 2 (£400) for the competition. That is a cost differential of £100 per forklift.

In summary, the purchase cost of our battery is £100 higher per forklift per year, but the energy savings are £280 per year. That means that our battery is a better value than that of our competitor's.

*Interviewer:* That is clearly an important result! What do we do with it?

**You:** We need to find a way to relay this information to the customer, because they apparently do not know about this benefit given our loss of market share. We may want to consider using a direct sales force to explain these benefits given the complexity. Printed materials may also be useful to describe the benefits in detail.

## Vault Bonus Case Analysis

The following issues would need to be covered for the candidate to have done an acceptable job:

I. What is the likely cause of decline? As addressed at the beginning of the case, the candidate needs to question whether the decline in sales is because of declining demand or declining market share.

2. What is the competitive outlook? You should at least recognize the need to examine competitive dynamics. As this case suggests, there are bound to be price differentials because of different labor rates.

3. What will be the price/volume relationship in the future? Pricing issues need to be considered.

Better answers might be more creative and include the following discussion points:

- The use of batteries and the corresponding energy savings

- Besides a discussion of promotion, some analysis of other areas in the value chain where costs could be reduced. This is critical since the consumers need to be educated about the fact that the client's products are superior not only in terms of overall quality but all also offer a better value for the money.

- Identification of creative, innovative methods in marketing as well as the possible risks

This case demonstrates some important aspects of a successful case interview, including collecting all the relevant information through effective questions and thinking through calculations and analysis out loud. In addition, while it's nice to be quick on your feet in making simple calculations, there are not many numbers to play with, and the interviewer is mostly looking at your ability to logically interpret whatever you can from the information provided. Try to extract all the information the interviewer possibly knows, and make and verbalize suitable assumptions wherever necessary.

# Case 15: Entertain Us

> The CEO of a large diversified entertainment corporation (XYZ) has asked our consulting firm to examine the operations of a subsidiary of his corporation that manufactures video game systems. Specifically, he needs to know whether he should approve a $200 million capital request for tripling the division's capacity. You are a member of the team assigned to this project. Assume you and I are at the first team meeting. What are the critical issues we should plan to examine to determine if the industry is an attractive one for continued investment and why?

*The primary issues of the case are to determine if the industry is attractive and especially if the client's position in that industry is sustainable. The questions you ask must aim to give you a clear idea of the structure of the industry and the company's competitive position in the industry. Here we will use the external/internal structure. Also note that you are being asked to identify the issues that are necessary for assessing both the industry and the client's position, but not explicitly solve the problem.*

**You:** First, I'd like to look at the external market situation. Important categories here include the current and potential players, customers, market size and share, sales and pricing. Then, I'd like to assess things internally at XYZ. What resource constraints do we have? At the end, I'd like to pull it together and summarize the top issues and opportunities that I think we will need to attack.

*Interviewer:* That sounds fine.

**You.** Let's begin with some external analysis. Who are the current players in the market, what is the current size of the market, and how much share does XYZ hold in that market?

*Interviewer:* There are three main players in the market. The XYZ division, though a relatively new entrant into the market, is the third-largest manufacturer of hardware in the industry with 10 percent market share. The top two producers. Boom and Game Fun, have 40 percent and 35 percent market share, respectively. The remainder is divided among small producers. The division sells to a broad range of consumers.

**You.**           You mention hardware. I assume you mean the systems on which computer games are played Does XYZ's division make games, or software?

*Interviewer:*  You're correct about what I mean about hardware. No, XYZ does not make games, or other software.

*The fact that the other two firms have 75 percent of the market may make it difficult for the division to gain market share and justify increasing capacity. Why does the division have only 10 percent market share?*

**You:**           What else do we know about the major competitors?

*Interviewer:*  Both of the two leaders make video games, in addition to the hardware. Also, they set the industry's hardware standards, and our client simply adapts to them.

**You:**           And who are the customers? Have new customer segments been identified?

*Interviewer:*  The division estimates that much of the initial target market — young families — has now purchased video game hardware. No large new user segments have been identified.

**You:**           How do the products reach the end customer?

*Interviewer:*  The primary outlets of distribution are electronics stores.

**You:**           Do we have an estimate of the annual sales of the industry in general and that of XYZ? What is the general trend?

*Interviewer:*  Well, we know that XYZ's sales have increased over last year from a relatively small base. We currently estimate annual sales of 500,000 units.

*Since you already know that the total market share of XYZ is 10 percent you can infer that the current estimate of industry sales is about 5,000,000 units annually.*

                In contrast, although overall industry growth has historically been strong, industry-wide sales growth has slowed in recent months.

*This could be attributed to lower demand of video games because of the prevailing economic conditions, and you might later test this assumption through discussions with the marketing department.*

*You:*           What are sales like in the current market? Have sales slowed for both hardware and game software?

*Interviewer:*  Over the last few years, we have noticed that software, or video game sales, have increased, while hardware, or game system, sales have decreased.

*You:*           What is the price for the basic unit? And how much do our competitors charge?

*Interviewer:*  The division's current sales price for the basic unit is $150. The competition charges less, but we don't have specifics on that right now.

*You:*           OK, I believe I have the major external context now. Let's move internally to XYZ itself and start with costs. What can you tell me about the different kinds of costs for the division?

*Interviewer:*  The main costs are components, assembly and labor. The division estimates that the current cost of production is $120, which includes the costs of marketing and promotion. The requested capacity expansion should reduce the cost by 5 to 7 percent and triple the production of the hardware units. We also know that the top two competitors have an estimated 10 to 15 percent cost advantage at the present time.

*You:*           How profitable is the company, and how significantly does the particular division contribute towards the margins?

*Interviewer:*  The division currently exceeds corporate return requirements, but profit margins have recently been falling. The sales of the division are slightly less than 20 percent of total XYZ sales.

*You:*           This would be a good time to identify what I think would be the top issues here.

*Interviewer:*  That sounds fine. Go ahead.

*Something doesn't seem quite right here. Why is XYZ interested in entering the market if it only has 10 percent of the market and if it doesn't make games for the system? Why is there any interest in the product at all? You'd better find out.*

*You:*           So our system costs more than our competitors.

Interviewer:  Yes.

*You:*           And sales are increasing, not decreasing?

*Interviewer:* That is correct.

*Think about it. Why would someone buy XYZ's hardware system if it's more expensive and has no dedicated software? Well, if it doesn't run its own games, it must run others. This gives you an idea.*

*You:* What software does XYZ's game system run?

*Interviewer:* XYZ's game hardware runs games from both its two top competitors, Game Fun and Boom.

*You:* Does Boom's hardware system run Game Fun's software, and vice versa?

*Interviewer:* No. Boom games are not compatible on Game Fun's hardware systems, and Game Fun games are unusable on Boom gaming systems.

*Now you know why XYZ' gaming systems are gaining market share. Video game users can play both Boom and Game Fun games on XYZ hardware. In fact, owners of Boom and Game Fun systems may be switching over to using XYZ hardware in order to enjoy games from both companies.*

*But before you recommend more resources go into XYZ's gaming division, you need to explore further — other possible sources of revenue, and possible competitors.*

*You:* Can XYZ make its own game software that works just on XYZ systems to provide an added incentive to buy XYZ hardware?

*Interviewer:* It's a possibility.

*You:* How about cloning Game Fun and/or Boom software? That may increase sales as well.

*Interviewer:* That's a possibility too.

*You:* Is it possible that Game Fun or Boom could change their hardware systems to render them capable of using the competitor's software?

*Interviewer:* It's possible, but unlikely.

*You:* Could another competitor emerge with hardware capable of running both Boom and Game Fun games?

*Interviewer:* It is possible, but it would take at least a $100 million investment.

*This is a fairly high barrier to entry. It seems that XYZ has a unique competitive advantage that is worth financing.*

**You:**     Even though software is a growth market and hardware is not, it seems that the fact that XYZ hardware can run a wider range of software (i.e., games) is a major competitive advantage. It seems unlikely that a competitor to XYZ will emerge in the near future. I would recommend making the investment. XYZ should also explore the idea of developing its own software that runs only on XYZ to further enhance its competitive position.

## Vault Bonus Case Analysis

The following are some of the top issues that you could lay out at this point (you don't need to describe all of these):

### I. External

Market health: You will want to question the continuation of overall industry growth and estimate the industry volume going forward. You will want to investigate market saturation, competitive or substitute products (such as home computers and high-end handhelds), and declining "per capita" usage. You should also question the feasibility of new products in a tight market. Finally, you will want to have some understanding of the price/volume relationship going forward.

Competitive outlook: You will want to further examine competitive dynamics. Issue areas might include concentration of market shares, control of retail channels, and R&D capabilities (which would impact the rate of new product introduction).

Capturing market share: If you were to triple capacity, where would the new customers come from? How would you steal share from your competitors if you didn't grow the market? Could you partner with, or buy, other video game software companies and create brand loyalty? Because the product purchasing mix seems to be shifting towards software, could you reduce your investment in hardware somewhat and invest in software? Your team will want to research possible new lines of business for the division, particularly in video games or some other revenue stream.

## II. Internal

Costs and Margins: Your team will want to understand the reasons for the poor profit performance of the division. In a manufacturing industry like this, you want to look closely at the supply chain, as you might be able to improve the costs of procurement of components and streamline the design and development cycles. Perhaps you will do a competitive intelligence study and determine just why the cost position of the competition is better. Finally, how will the capacity expansion impact the division's bottom line? Where, exactly, in the value chain would we see the reduction of costs?

Capabilities: You will be interested in seeing if XYZ has the resources to expand and determine what else needs to happen within the company. For example, tripling the capacity implies hiring more sales personnel and additional quality control experts. What are the exact costs of expansion in terms of capital and ongoing operating expenses? How long would the expansion take? What is XYZ's policy with respect to required return on capital and payback period?

# Case 16: Raising the Roof on Credit

> Mike is the CEO of a credit card company known as BIG Bank. BIG Bank issues standard credit cards with a rate of 19 percent to prime-rated customers. For years, all of the company's competitors also issued cards with a 19 percent rate. However, now BIG Bank is faced with a challenge. Mike just read in this morning's newspaper that his biggest competitor, ABC Bank, has lowered its credit card rate to 15 percent. Mike immediately calls your consulting firm seeking a solution. As a consultant, what is your take?

*This case will likely require some number crunching, but you need a lot more information. A great way to approach a case like this is to start with an appropriate general framework and work your way down to the calculations (likely some sort of break-even analysis or profitability impact calculation). Since we have some information about competition and customers, we will start with the Four C's framework. Don't forget to state all of your assumptions clearly at the very outset, consider marketing and implementation issues, and provide suitable recommendations.*

*You:*      Well, I'm surprised Mike had to read about this change in the paper! Let's start with the competition, which seems to be the most important issue given ABC's announcement. Who are the other competitors in the market, and what are they expected to do?

*Interviewer:*      While there are many competitors, including banks and finance companies, BIG Bank and ABC Bank are the two biggest in the industry. Both are well entrenched in several regions throughout the country. The indications we have received so far is that no other competitors have reacted so far. In all likelihood, they are waiting for us to react in some manner before doing something on their own.

     *The CEO's reply implies that the rest of the competition is not a major concern at this stage, so you can effectively ignore that issue.*

*You:*      What are the financials of the competitor, ABC Bank?

*Interviewer:*      Specifics are not available. However, we know they are similar to BIG Bank. ABC's financial statements indicate similarity in cost structure.

*You can assume that a lot of the financial information you gather for BIG will apply to its competitor.*

**You:** Is ABC's credit card any different from the one that is offered by BIG Bank at 19 percent?

*Interviewer:* There are no substantial differences. Both of them offer similar benefits.

**You:** What other products does ABC Bank offer?

*Interviewer:* ABC's products are similar to ours.

**You:** That's probably enough information about the competition for now. Let's move on to the customer base. Who are the customers? Have you tried to target specific customer segments in different regions?

*Interviewer:* The customers are prime-rated credit card holders who maintain an average account balance of $2,000. There are 100,000 customers. We have not targeted any specific customer base.

**You:** While we're on the topic of customers, what can you tell me about the revenue BIG's customers generate? What other sources of revenue are there?

*Interviewer:* Interest on account balances is the only source of revenue.

**You:** Since we just talked about revenues, let's move into costs. What are the expenses of BIG Bank?

*Interviewer:* Cost of funds is 6 percent of average account balances, general and administrative expenses are 3 percent and losses are 4 percent.

**You:** Are there any immediate opportunities for cost reduction at BIG? Are there any economies of scale? Do the costs decrease when we get more customers?

*Interviewer:* We continuously look for cost reduction opportunities and there appear to be no significant opportunities at this time. No, there aren't any economies of scale.

**You:** That's a lot of useful information. Let's touch on capabilities before we move onto some calculations. What is our competitive situation in terms of systems and organizational structure?

*Interviewer:*   Both BIG and ABC use industry standard computer systems, and there is no opportunity for significant improvement in the time frame that will affect the pricing challenge. BIG Bank is building a data warehouse. As far as the organizational structure, ours is very similar to the one prevalent in the banking industry.

*You:*   What advertising and promotion campaigns are planned?

Interviewer:   The company periodically uses direct mail campaigns and will continue to do so. We send customers letters separately from their monthly statement.

*Since you now have most of the information, you should start providing recommendations based on all the information you have gathered. Although recommendations have to be very specific, it is always better to provide several alternatives.*

*You:*   All right, I would now like to take a couple of minutes to consolidate this information into a brief income statement. I would like to see how BIG's financials look at the 15 percent rate.

*Interviewer:*   That's fine. Take your time.

*You have a few ways to proceed at this point. You could present the information in the form of income statement tables or a straightforward P&L calculation. Moreover, you could take a moment to calculate things and then walk through them, or you could think through your calculations out loud for the interviewer.*

*You:*   Basically, there are two scenarios. The company can either hold rates steady at 19 percent or it can match the competitor's 15 percent rate. At 15 percent, we would lose revenue, but with a lower rate we would likely gain more customers. The question is how many. Based on the financial data, I have constructed a break-even analysis to determine how many customers we would need to retain our current level of income.

*At this point, walk your interviewer through your income statement line by line. Beware! Some interviewers will pretend to not know what an income statement is, so be prepared to explain the income statement with exhaustive simplicity.*

## BIG Bank Income Statement Analysis

| | | Hold at 19% | Match 15% Rate |
|---|---|---|---|
| Average Account Balance | | $2,000 | $2,000 |
| # of Customers | | 100,000 | 100,000 |
| Rate | | 19.0% | 15.0% |
| | | | |
| **Per Customer** | | | |
| Revenue | | $380 | $300 |
| Expenses | | | |
| Cost of Funds | 6% | $120 | $120 |
| G&A | 3% | $60 | $60 |
| Losses | 4% | $80 | $80 |
| Total Expenses | | $260 | $260 |
| Net Income per Customer | | $120 | $40 |
| Total Net Income | | $12,000,000 | $4,000,000 |
| | | | |
| Break-even number of customers | | 34% | |

**You:** We can see that at the current customer count, switching to the 15 percent rate would result in about 66 percent reduction in net income. Therefore, holding rates steady at 19 percent is more profitable for BIG unless more than 66 percent of BIG's customers leave. While BIG should obviously attempt to retain as many of its customers as possible, BIG Bank should be able to retain at least 34 percent of its customers to justify sticking with the 19 percent rate. I would recommend that BIG continue with the 19 percent rate while attempting to prevent customers from switching.

**Interviewer:** Those are some very interesting numbers, and your recommendation makes sense. But what are some ways we could prevent customers from switching to ABC? I bet that lower rate looks awfully appealing to most customers.

**You:** There are a number of ways you could attack the problem. For example, opportunities could be identified using customer data to promote other BIG Bank products or products offered through strategic alliances with other companies. Promotional campaigns could be targeted at customers who are likely to carry a revolving balance. Promotional campaigns can also be carried out through the company web site or through your partners' web sites. Other data-based marketing opportunities include customized mailings based on past spending habits, pre-approved loans based on life events such as marriage, birth of children and home purchase.

*Interviewer:* Those sound expensive.

**You:** They can be, but there are ways to accomplish this at reasonable costs. For example, direct mailing involves additional expenditure in terms of postage costs and materials, so it would be better to have statement inserts, those little slips of paper we put inside customers' monthly statements, which they return to us when they mail us their payments. Statement messages, a line or two of text typed on the remittance stub of each statement, might be effective as well.

*Interviewer:* Those are good ideas. What else?

**You:** Over the long term, the company should consider using its data warehouse as a competitive advantage to segment its customer base and target those customers who are likely to be loyal. It's possible that ABC is doing the same thing, so we might want to start this process in the near future. Data warehouse technology can also be used to mitigate risk by targeting customers who are unlikely to default. That said, while the data warehouse can be a competitive advantage, it will not solve the immediate challenge of a competitor who just lowered its price. But it will definitely provide information on how many customers will remain loyal to BIG Bank or switch to ABC Bank.

In addition, the company could diversify its product line by offering products to customers in different segments such as sub-prime borrowers and students. It could also offer Gold and Platinum cards to differentiate customers. Other benefits like airline miles, temporarily low APRs on transfers from other cards to BIG and auto insurance could be offered to retain loyal customers and lure new ones.

# Case 17: A Matter of Coating

Our client produces a range of synthetic materials in varying widths and lengths. Each material is used for packaging, but differs in costs, weight, flexibility, and general performance. Each material can be coated with any one of four or five types of chemical coating which make the materials more or less impervious to heat, light, water, vapor, etc. All of the machines that makes these materials are housed in a single factory. Each machine is capable of running any one of the various materials and/or coating combinations. The client does not wish to invest in additional equipment at this time.

The client has asked us what combination of products he should run to increase his plant's profitability. How would you go about determining the optimal mix of potential products using these machines?

*The profit of the plant will be maximized when the most profitable product mix is produced and sold. You should cover differences for each product in terms of the two components of profitability: revenues (market demand, market share and corresponding prices) and expenses (fixed and variable manufacturing and selling costs).*

**You:** Let's first look at the revenue side of things. First, what kind of products does the company manufacture?

**Interviewer:** Our client's machinery can produce hundreds of different products. Some are uniquely made to meet specific customer requirements, while others are used by a wide variety of customers.

**You:** And who are the client's customers?

**Interviewer:** Our client's customers are primarily consumers or industrial product manufacturers who use the synthetic materials in packaging their own products.

**You:** How are the products priced?

**Interviewer:** Each product's price is dependent on both the client's cost to manufacture it as well as the market for the product.

*You:*        Let's touch on competition, as it impacts revenue. How many players are currently in the market? And how much market share does the client have?

*Interviewer:*  The industry is highly fragmented. Several small manufacturers supply similar products to a range of customers. Our client estimates he has less than 1 percent of the total market. No competitor has more than 3 percent of the total market

*You:*        OK, let's move on to expenses now. What can you tell me about the fixed and variable manufacturing costs for the products?

*Interviewer:*  The cost to manufacture is dependent on the materials used and the manufacturing process. Of course, some of the costs are fixed and some are variable.

*You:*        Who supplies the material inputs?

*Interviewer:*  Our client primarily uses commodity products in the manufacturing process. All can be obtained from a number of sources.

## Vault Bonus Case Analysis

Why no conclusion? Note that the information gathered so far is general, especially in terms of the products, price and costs. This could mean that the interviewer is not looking for a specific answer, but is more concerned with whether you are going in the right track in tackling the issue at hand. Often, if you digress from the main topic, the interviewer will guide you back to the central issue. In this case, if you are discussing issues which are not relevant to the profitability of each product line or to maximizing the profitability of the plant, the interviewer might repeat the question and ask how the issue being discussed will lead to a solution for the client.

**You should, at a minimum, address the following issues:**

**1.** Are there market limitations to the potential production of any one material? (You should be in a position to discuss or ask questions if any particular product has any specific peculiarities in terms of weight, flexibility, or performance, and if special care needs to be taken to address these issues.)

**2.** What kind of competition exists for these products? (If there is competition, how is it affecting the manufacturing process? Is there any impact of competition on the other components of the value chain?)

**3.** What are the differences in costs in the manufacturing of these materials? For example, do some coatings cost more than others? Do some materials have inherent cost differences?

**4.** Is there flexibility in the pricing of these products? Can any product be marked lower or higher than the rest?

**Additional observations should include:**

**1.** Are there differences in the setup time and costs when switching between materials or coatings? (Since a machine can handle several different products, are there any special considerations that would need to be addressed?)

**2.** Do these materials move at different speeds through the machines? (This is necessary to determine if there is a lag in the process, and if one product must wait until another is finished.)

**3.** How interchangeable are the machines? Are some machines better suited toward one product or another?

**4.** Is there unlimited market demand for these products?

**5.** Are there technological displacement or replacement products on the horizon? (If there are, could it be a better option for the client to upgrade the machines/technologies, rather than making a completely new investment on another machine?)

A truly outstanding answer would formulate a profit maximization algorithm maximizing the profit contribution per machine hour.

**1.** Profit contribution is unit volume times unit price less variable cost. (You can come up with a suitable number in order to do the calculation, but just mentioning the process in most cases is more than sufficient. Remember you typically don't have more than 30 minutes for a case.)

**2.** Machine-hour capacity is a surrogate for fixed costs per unit of volume. Fixed costs take into account depreciation and standby costs, as well as those costs that are independent of the variable costs per pound or ton produced.

**An outstanding answer might also include:**

- Recognition of the asset costs and implied capital, as well as the income or profit contribution

- The potentially substantial differences in volume produced per machine-hour and/or the price obtainable in the market and competitive actions

- Possible risk mitigation opportunities (for example, a plan of action if there is a breakdown in the machinery)

# Case 18: Can't Be Beet

A small biotech company has come up with a revolutionary new seed for sugar beets that are exactly the same as regular beets but yield twice as much sugar. The company wishes to sell the patent (which is valid for twenty years) so that the inventors can pay off their venture capitalists and retire to an island with lots of sun and palm trees. What is the value of the patent?

*The price of a product is determined by the market. Let's assume that there are no inputs for the new seed technology (it's already produced and can simply be cloned), and that agricultural goods are commodities sold to a dispersed market of buyers who, individually, exercise little power over the price. The price, then, will be based on the value of the product to the buyer, and on competition from similar and substitute goods. Since this is a patented product, there are no similar goods, and therefore no alternate seed sources.*

**You:** What are other potential substitutes and are there any peculiarities for these products?

*Interviewer:* Substitute goods are regular sugar beet seeds and possibly seeds for sugar cane.

**You:** Why not grow sugar cane?

*Interviewer:* Sugar cane is grown in entirely different climates and is not considered to be a competing product in this market.

**You** That rules out one possibility and makes the solution easier. The only possible competition is from regular sugar beet seeds. The value of that product should be compared to the value of our new seeds. In order to be grown into beets, seeds require land and labor. The farmer using our new seeds has two possibilities: he can grow twice as much sugar with the same amount of land and labor or he can grow the same amount of sugar with half the land and labor, since the yield of the new beet is twice that of the old one. Let's look just at land for simplicity here.

*Interviewer:* Do you believe the farmer can sell twice as much sugar?

**You:** One individual farmer in a commodities market should be able to sell all his increased output at the market price, but if every farmer uses the new technology and doubles his output, the price will have to fall. The question then becomes whether the demand for sugar is elastic. Using common sense, would you expect anyone to consume more sugar (bake more cookies or make more lemonade) when the price of sugar drops? Probably not, because sugar is already a pretty cheap staple product and rarely the most expensive ingredient in something. You might want to think about other uses for sugar such as making alcohol to use as a substitute for gasoline. This market's demand would probably be elastic.

*Interviewer:* That is a good point, but let's assume demand for sugar is fixed for now.

*This is an example of a clue where the interviewer does not want you to pursue this any further. In most case interviews, the interviewer usually gives subtle hints that will indicate to the candidate that either he/she is digressing from the topic at hand or is delving too deep into the subject and it probably goes beyond the scope of the interview. Having established these facts, get back to the original line of the argument and continue.*

*You:* If demand for sugar is fixed, then the only possibility for the farmer is to use only half the land to grow the same amount of sugar. So now you need to determine the value of the land saved. This could be determined by the market price of agricultural land times the area saved.

*Interviewer:* Selling the land is a bit of a problem. There is a glut of land available, and it is unlikely that the farmers will be able to sell their land at all within a period of a few years.

*Oops! Now what? Another possibility is to see if the farmer may have other uses for the land.*

*You:* Can he grow a different crop?

*Interviewer:* It is possible to grow other crops on that type of soil. For instance, cabbage grows well in those types of climates. The problem is that the profit margins on cabbage are only 20 percent of those on sugar beets.

It seems that the farmers will not derive a whole lot of benefit from the new seeds. You have looked at the end consumers of refined sugar and at the producers of the beets now.

**You:**       What other players could possibly benefit from the new invention?

*A good way to approach this is to use a value chain or process flow.*

*Interviewer*   Why don't you tell me?

**You:**       How does the sugar finally reach the consumer?

*Interviewer:*  Sugar beets are produced by the farmer and then shipped to the sugar refinery by truck. The sugar refinery makes sugar crystals from the beets and packages them. The packaged sugar is then shipped to retailers, where it is distributed to the end consumer.

The sugar that reaches the end consumer is the same sugar and in the same amount that would be shipped if old seeds were used. Because, the transportation process involved in both the cases is the same, there are no cost savings there. From the farmer to the refinery, however, the amount of beets shipped would be only half the traditional amount. As a result, trucking expenses should drop by 50 percent.

**You:**       Will the refinery realize any production benefits from the reduced number of beets?

*Interviewer:*  As it turns out, the processing cost of the new beets will be 25% percent higher per beet than the old ones.

**You:**       If the number of beets is reduced by 50 percent and the cost per new beet is only 25 percent higher, there will be a 25 percent production cost savings to the refinery. The refinery should be willing to pay the farmer a higher price for the new beets. The total savings from the new seeds can be summed up as follows: farmers gain 10 percent on their profit margins from growing cabbage on half their land. Here's why: Because profit margins on cabbage are only 20 percent that of beets, 20 percent on half the land equals 10 percent. Trucking expenses from the farmer to the refinery are cut by 50 percent and production costs are reduced by 25 percent. Next we should find out how much each step contributes to the final price of sugar.

*Interviewer:*  Growing the sugar is 40 percent of the cost, trucking 10 percent, refining 30 percent, and distribution 20 percent.

**You:**       The savings are 10% x 40% = 4% in growing; 50% x 10% = 5% in trucking; and 25% x 30% = 7.5% in refining. This adds up to a total savings of 16.5%. Multiply this number by the annual sugar demand and you get a dollar value of annual savings.

*Interviewer:* How would you estimate the annual demand for sugar?

*At this point you drop your head in exhaustion for you will have to do an estimation case within a business case. In a typical case interview, unless it is a specific estimation example, you can come up with a suitable assumption. For example, in this case, you can assume that the resulting figure is $3 billion. You can briefly explain to the interviewer how you arrived at the number — an explanation is given in the sidebar below.*

The value of the patent is the net present value of 20 years (the length of the patent) of 16.5% x $3 billion, which I estimate to be the annual demand of sugar.

## Estimating the annual demand for sugar in the United States

In estimation cases you are asked to come up with an "educated guess" of some number, such as the all-time classic: "How much does a Boeing 747 weigh?" While the questions may sometimes seem "off the wall," this is an important skill to possess in consulting work. As a consultant, you will often have to make decisions based on incomplete or unavailable data, which makes it important to generate reasonable estimates.

In these types of exercises it is not important whether your assumptions are right or wrong (in the real world you have a research department to find that out for you), but make sure that your estimates are at least reasonable based on common sense. For example, if one of the assumptions you make is about the U.S. population, do not say that you assume it is 10 million.

It is important that you use easy numbers for your assumptions because you will have to do some arithmetic off the top of your head. If you start out with an estimate of the U.S. population of 237 million, you will probably start sweating profusely when you have to divide or multiply this number. Using 250 or 300 million is a lot easier to work with.

Estimation problems are based on logical reasoning applied to a number of known data points (your assumptions, which would be known data points had they been researched) to arrive at the desired answer. Because your logic is what is tested, lay it out clearly for the interviewer. Before you start making assumptions, tell the interviewer how you are going to logically figure out the answer. Once you have done that, make the assumptions and do the math. Make sure, however, that you do not make the problem too complicated. If you have a reasonable idea of the numbers, go with the assumption and start filling in the equations.

Also remember that since most of us are used to calculators and don't often add up large strings of numbers in our heads, it is useful to practice your arithmetic. Calculators are generally not allowed, and it can be quite embarrassing to stumble on a simple calculation in an interview. This danger is especially prevalent since you will probably be a bit nervous, and thus less able to think clearly. The only way to get better at it is by practice; lots of it.

Coming back to our question of the annual demand for sugar, we start with the basic assumption of the number of people in the US.

There are 300 million people in the U.S. It's fair to assume that all of them consume sugar in some form or the other. Let's assume that in an average family of four typically consumes 18 or 20 five-pound bags of sugar per year, for a total of 80 to 100 pounds of sugar per year. So the demand per person per year is about 20 pounds. It may be higher for some and lower for other, but 20 is a pretty reasonable average. With 300 million people, if 20 pounds is consumed per person, then the annual demand will be approximately 6 billion pounds.

If you've ever been to the grocery store, you know that a 5-pound pack of sugar costs around $2.50 – an average of $.50/lb. Using this value we can calculate the dollar value of the annual demand of sugar in the U.S. to be around 6 billion pounds x $.50 per pound, or $3 billion.

## Vault Bonus Case Analysis

As a successful consultant you will have to:

**1.** Collect all the relevant information by asking questions. A case interview is typically an interactive process, and most likely the interviewer will volunteer additional information as the interview progresses or when you ask questions. It is important to gather as much information as you need. Try and extract all the information the interviewer possibly knows. Make suitable assumptions wherever necessary.

**2.** Some general knowledge also helps. Common sense (especially in the estimation cases) is very important.

**3.** Because of the complexity of some cases (like this one — where one may lose track of the path being followed) you will be presented with, it may not be possible to get to the point where you start making suggestions for improvements in the time frame allotted. This does not matter, as long as you demonstrated your ability to think clearly and to apply the correct business tools to get to the causes of the problem. The firm probably took weeks rather than just thirty minutes to get to the point where you stopped in the interview. Just summarize what you have found out up to that point, and how you would proceed with your analysis if you'd had the time.

# APPENDIX

# Consulting Glossary

Consultants often lapse into their own lingo while conversing with civilians, thus further panicking those who were unaware that they possessed something called a "skill set" (for what it's worth, the things that you're good at). Following is a basic list that can raise your level of familiarity with consulting terms that consultants like to fling about in case interviews:

**Bananagram:** A graph showing profitability (the typical measure of profitability for this graph is return on capital employed, or "ROCE" [pronounced roachy]) vs. relative market share. The graph shows that the higher the market share, the higher the profitability.

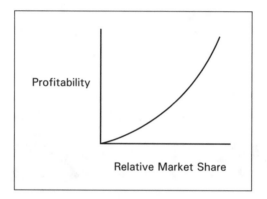

**BCG matrix:** A portfolio assessment tool developed by BCG. Also called a growth/share matrix.

**Benchmarking:** Measuring a value or practice or other business measure (such as costs) against other companies in the industry.

**Blank slide:** Initial sketch on paper for a slide to be used in a consulting case presentation (called blank because it does not include data until analysts put it in).

**Brainteaser:** A type of consulting interview question in which the job seeker is asked to solve a logic problem.

**Business Process Re-engineering (BPR):** BPR is the process of reviewing a client's business processes, eliminating unneeded or "non-value-added" tasks, and then implementing the leaner, more efficient process.

**Case team:** Team that works on a consulting project for a client. Usually composed of one partner (or director), one consultant, and two or more analysts.

**Change management:** One of the services provided by consulting firms, in which the firm helps a company cope with a period of significant change (such as a merger, downsizing or restructuring).

**Consultancy:** A typically European name for what we call a "consulting firm" in the U.S., though the term has picked up currency in the U.S.

**Convergence:** The trend toward industries uniting. (For example, cable TV customers may someday be able to place telephone calls using cable technology, while telephone customers may be able to receive television through phone lines.)

**Core competencies:** The areas in which a company excels. Consultants believe a company should enter only those businesses which are part of its core competencies.

**Critical path:** This term comes from Operations Management theory. Every business process is made up of a series of tasks. Some of these tasks are related to maintenance of the process or administrative and bookkeeping issues. Taken away, they do not directly impact the end result of the business process. If you eliminate these non-meaningful tasks, you are left with the core set of tasks that must occur in order for the process to produce the desired result. This is the critical path. In everyday consulting language, it is used to refer to only those work tasks which are the most important at the time.

**Customer Relationship Management (CRM):** Term that refers to the data-gathering methods used to collect information about a client's customers. Usually focuses on sales force automation, customer service/call center, field service, and marketing automation.

**DCF: (Discounted Cash Flow).** The present value of a future cash flow.

**Drilldown:** Asking questions to gather more detail about a situation, usually from a high-level (big picture) view.

**80/20 rule:** A consultant's rule of thumb about time management. Getting 80 percent of the answer you're looking for will take 20 percent of your time. The other 20 percent of the answer (80 percent of your time) is probably not worth it.

**Engagement:** A consulting assignment received by a consulting firm. Also called a "case" or "project."

**Enterprise Resource Planning (ERP):** Processes or software that help streamline departments or divisions of a company.

**Experience curve:** The principle that a company's costs decline as its production increases. One assumption used by consultants is that a company's costs decline by roughly 25 percent for every doubling in production (e.g. a company's 200th unit of a product costs 75 percent of the 100th unit's cost).

**Granularity:** This simply refers to the basic elements that make up a business problem. Imagine a handful of sand. At a high level it's simply a handful of sand; at a granular level it is bits of many different kinds of rock and shell matter reduced to fine granules over time by the action of the ocean. Consultants are not usually this poetic.

**Guesstimate:** A type of consulting interview question. Guesstimates require job seekers to make an educated estimate of something (often the size of the market for a particular product or service) using basic calculations.

**Helicoptering:** See High-level view.

**High-level view:** This is also referred to as a "50,000-foot view." It refers to describing a situation in general terms or as an overview of a situation.

**Hoteling:** Consultants move around so much that in some firms they are not assigned permanent offices, just a voice mail extension. Each week, they must call up the office nearest them to request a desk. This is called "hoteling."

**Hurdle rate:** A company's cost of capital. In general, if the return on an investment exceeds this "hurdle rate," the company should make the investment; otherwise, the company should not.

**Implementation:** The process by which a consulting firm ensures that the advice it gives to a client company is enacted.

**Learning curve:** The rate at which a consultant acquires background information or industry knowledge needed for a case. A "steep" curve is a good thing.

**NPV: (Net present value).** The sum of a series of discounted cash flows. Used to assess the profitability for a client of making an investment or undertaking a project.

**O'Hare test:** A test consultants use in interviews to assess personality "fit." If I was stuck overnight with this person at O'Hare airport, would I have fun?

**On the beach:** For consultants, the spare time between assignments, when their work hours decline drastically. Consultants between assignments are said to be "on the beach" (not literally). This expression originated at McKinsey.

**Out-of-the-box thinking:** Creativity.

**Outsourcing:** Taking a process normally performed within a company and hiring an outside vendor to perform the task, often at a lower cost and with better results. Examples of processes that are commonly outsourced include: payroll, data processing, recruitment and document processing. Outsourcing is a growing trend among corporations.

**Reengineering:** A largely discredited fad of the early 1990s, which advocates a complete overhaul (and usually downsizing) of a company's strategies, operations, and practices.

**Rightsize:** Also "downsize," this is just a kinder, friendlier term for restructuring the elements of a company. This is most often used in reference to headcount reductions, but can apply to plants, processes, technology, financial elements and office locations.

**Shareholder value:** The wealth of a company's stockholders or their equity (ownership) in the company. The primary goal of consultants in undertaking any engagement is to increase shareholder value.

**Stakeholder:** A critical person who has a stake in the outcome of a particular situation. Most commonly, the stakeholders in a case are the shareholders creditors or employees.

**Total Quality Management:** Also known as TQM. Management with the purpose or intent of producing a product or offering a service of the highest quality, with zero tolerance for defects.

**Value migration:** The flow of economic and shareholder value away from obsolete business models to new, more effective designs.

**Value-added:** Used to define a service or product in a marketplace that adds value to a pre-existing product or way of doing things.

**Workplan:** A schedule for completing a consulting engagement.

**Writing a deck:** Preparing slides for presentations to clients.

**White space opportunity:** An opportunity for a company to make money in an area in which they are currently generating zero revenue (for example, launching a new product line, licensing an existing brand or technology, or entering a new geographic market).

# About the Authors

**Jim Slepicka:** Jim's career as a "creative problem-solver" began early, trouble-shooting operational challenges on the family farm. A strong believer in combining hands-on, practical experience with theoretical academic training, Jim ran his own business during high school and worked aboard for a year during college, traveling throughout Central & Eastern Europe and assisting the Czech Royal Family on consolidation of assets restituted after the Velvet Revolution (including several castles, a winery, brewery, spa and mineral water company).

Maintaining a focus on market-strategy issues, Jim's consulting experience has included roles with The Aberdeen Group, BP-Amoco Corporation, and most recently, PricewaterhouseCoopers' Strategic Change practice.

Jim is currently Co-Founder and President of Product Animations, Inc. and is a graduate of Harvard University and University of Chicago Graduate School of Business.

**Rajit Malhotra:** Rajit's first entrepreneurial foray was at the age of seven helping his mother with her poultry business. Since then he's been implicated in a series of startups, both his own, and those he helped found. He sold his first company, a building materials retail and distribution business, after running it for five years. He also founded the venture capital firm, August Holding, as a vehicle to assist Indian entrepreneurs establish their ventures. Rajit is currently at the management consulting firm, McKinsey & Company. He is a graduate of the Wharton School (1994), Kellogg School of Management (2002) and the Kennedy School at Harvard University (2002).

**Srikant Balan:** Srikant began his consulting career with Tata Consultancy Services (TCS a division of TATA Sons, the largest conglomerate in India). As a Technology consultant he was involved in the setting up of the first depository (National Securities & Depository) in India. He consulted several companies in the US from 1999. To supplement his engineering degree earned in 1996 from India, he took a year's sabbatical to earn a Master's Degree in Business Administration from University of Pittsburgh (2001). He is currently consulting for a software company (Group 1 Software) in the Washington DC area. An avid traveler, Srikant also has a deep interest in films besides being a very passionate follower of the game of cricket.

**Deborah Liu** began her consulting career at Boston Consulting Group after earning her B.S.E. in Civil/Environmental Engineering from Duke University. She has consulted for clients a variety of industries including energy and utilities, consumer goods, financial services and non-profit. Her experience is also enhanced by her internships at Procter & Gamble, Ford Motor Company, and eBay. A recent graduate of the Stanford Graduate Schoolof Business, Deborah spent the summer during business school working for the Hong Kong office for McKinsey & Company. Currently, Deborah works at PayPal in Product Management.